Gisela Elisabeth Heinz, Peter Kutzki

Messages from the Shroud of Turin

Gisela Elisabeth Heinz, Peter Kutzki

Messages from the Shroud of Turin

Mystery and Emblem for Our Day

John 14:9
Jesus answered, "Don't you know me, Philip? I have been among
you such a long time! Anyone who has seen Me has seen the Father.
So how can you say, 'Show us the Father'?

2021

Bibliographic Information from the German National Library
(Deutsche Nationalbibliothek)
This publication is listed by the German National Library in the German National
Bibliography; detailed bibliographic data is available on the Internet at
http://dnb.d-nb.de.

1st Edition 2021

English translation: Dr. Cynthia Dyre, Leipzig
Cover image: 59957338 / imago images / United Archives International
Cover design: Robert Herzig / Kunst & Kunstcoaching, Hurlach
Layout: Verlagsservice Monika Rohde, Leipzig
Printer and Publisher: BoD – Books on Demand, Norderstedt

ISBN 9783752660128

Table of Contents

Author's Foreword

*"Tell me to whom you pray when things are going well and
I will tell you how devout you are."*
Kurt Tucholski

Dear Reader,

Thank you very much for your interest in this book. Please allow me to briefly introduce myself to you and to explain a little about my intentions in writing this book.

My parents saw to it that I was baptized and raised in the Christian faith. Even as a child, I loved the image of Jesus set in the stained-glass window in the chancel of our church. In my youth, however, I became an atheist and, later on, in the prevailing atmosphere that dominated Germany during the 1968 student movement, I became an esotericist. In the late 1970s, I studied Dentistry, going on to become a licensed dentist with my own practice in the German city of Hamburg. But, my belief in Christ never completely disappeared.

It happened during a period in my life when I had the feeling I was in my personal prime – all of the plans I had made in my youth had come to fruition. I had attained the majority of my goals and had the means to lead the kind of life I chose. One day, as I was sitting in my car on the way home from work, I heard a compelling inner voice say to me emphatically: „There is a God!" This happened at a time during which I was searching for the meaning of life. I came across a book titled "The Lord Speaks." In it, I read for the first time about mysticism: it was a compilation of the writings of Jakob Lorber. The topics included Jesus, God, creation, and the universe. These writings helped me rediscover my inner spiritual connection to Jesus Christ. The texts have been given the generic name "The New Revelation." They provide an explanation of Christianity and the connection between our earthly reality and the Eternal. The mysteries into which Christ initiated his mystics are convincing to me. For some who are seeking God, the language in which the texts have been written may seem outdated and distracting, but the prophets could only describe the events and principles revealed by them in the language of their times. The texts of the New Revelation allow the reader to experience the orderly

Christian perspective of life and to have the sense of being an eyewitness to the life of Jesus. The messages it conveys are all imbued with expressions of Christ's overwhelming love for us.

In many cases, people only discover God when they are confronted with a personal emergency. I was lucky, in that, in many ways, I was doing quite well during this time. One of the things I enjoyed doing in my free time was reading interesting non-fiction books. My greatest interest at that time was in learning about Jesus Christ. One day, while out shopping in Hamburg, I happened upon the booklet "Das Tuch" (*"The Shroud"*) by Oswald Scheuermann. Even just reading the preface of the book, I found myself fascinated, as I learned about the most recent results of his research on the Shroud of Turin.

Soon afterwards, I discovered a clear reference to the Shroud of Turin in the Abgarus Letter written by the mystic, Jakob Lorber. I subsequently discovered that some of the texts in the New Revelation confirmed the authenticity of the Shroud. In the meantime, motivated by my love for my husband, who has since passed away, I left Hamburg to move to Germany's southernmost federal state, Bavaria.

For many years now, it has been my wish to provide as many people as possible with an undistorted view of the historical Jesus. I wish to share with others the joy and gratitude I feel for His[1] love and the confidence I have in a future grounded in Him. With this book, I would like to share with you, dear reader, and all those who seek God, my insights, which were gained over the course of many years, into Christ's Shroud of Turin.

Initially, I was not planning to write a book. The notes I took during a period of more than thirty years were originally only intended as a reinforcement my faith. The unfortunate disadvantage to this is that I did not always document my references. The transference of my notes into this book therefore sometimes reflects an approximate reconstruction of the information I collected over the years.

What I found particularly interesting were comparisons between the New Revelation and current scientific findings on the macro- and microcosm. Generally speaking, our modern understanding of the nature of the universe, made possible through the use of telescopes, and in particular, the Hubble Space Telescope, does not at all contradict the insights I have gained from mysticism.

For instance, in the New Revelation, Jakob Lorber explains that, in reality, throughout the universe and on Earth, no matter actually exists, but only "aligned spirit" or "frozen light." Decades after Lorber, this scientific manifestation was confirmed by modern research conducted by renowned particle physicists. One of Nobel Prize laureate Max Planck's scientific discoveries demonstrates that matter truly does not exist. What we humans recognize as matter consists, as it were, of energy fields that have no mass. The scientific discoveries that have been honored with the Nobel Prize for Physics have increased my enthusiasm for the New Revelation. I have confidence in the future, because in Lorber's writings, Jesus prophesies to his disciples concerning the time to come[2]:

> Only in the end will all superstition be swept off the ground of earth with the weapons of the sciences and arts, without in any way interfering with man's free will. Through this in time there will well be a complete void of faith among men; but such a state will only last a very short time. (GGJ 9, 89, 9–11)

> But this will not remain so; in the right moment I will awaken men for the pure sciences and technologies, and these will proclaim it from the rooftops to men, how the servants of Balaam[3] have performed their miracles. Through this, pure science in all things and also the pure arts will become an invincible forerunner and champion for Me against the old superstitions; and when the Augean stables will be purified by that, then I will have an easy and most effective return to this earth. Because My purest teaching of life will unite easily with the pure science of men and give men a complete light of life, because one purity can never pollute the other, as one sunlit truth cannot pollute the other. (GGJ 9, 90, 11)

My faith was further reinforced in 2017, when we traveled to Ravenna, Italy and viewed the early Christian mosaic art found in that city. Here, golden shimmering images portray a peacefully mystical world – one in which evil has found no quarter. The monumental depictions of the cross in the starry sky express the symbolic content of the cross in a uniquely beautiful way (see Figure 22, p. 97).

The challenge of defining the Trinity, which I discuss in the third chapter, is also clearly recognizable In Ravenna's history, including the religious disputes associated with it. As I was writing the book, it was important to me that my readers, in their search for truth and God, would, in confidence and with a heart free of fear, be able to discover the Word of God and His face. If we are to understand our religion in a loving way, one crucial element is to properly and fully understand the crucifixion of Christ.

This Crucifixion, carried out by humans, was a monstrous cruelty, which God indeed allowed, but which was never demanded of Him. It was the cruel testing of Jesus' divinity by human beings. To my mind, it is time to allow the inhumane crime of Jesus' crucifixion, including all depictions of it, fade into history. Instead, let us turn to the risen, living, and omnipresent Christ and His universal symbol: the cross (also see GGJ 8, 149, 5 ff.).

The message revealed by Christ's shroud is that, with the Crucifixion, God was willing to make the most extreme sacrifice imaginable for the sake of our immortal souls. He endured this martyrdom so that we would be able to evolve freely, because human beings can only become true children of God if their free will and love for God are allowed to develop independently of any external pressure.

Following His crucifixion, Jesus rose from the dead with a spiritual body, and with His shroud, left us material evidence of the existence of the spiritual world. For His followers, His resurrection and the manifestations of His spiritual body were an indispensable confirmation of His teachings. With these, he also affirmed to them the truth of His statement: „My Kingdom is not of this world." (John 18:36)[4]

The Shroud carries a message of its own for our science-driven times. It provides us with numerous clues about and helpful approaches to the message of Jesus. We have been given this as a material sign of God's power to spiritually and physically resurrect the dead. Jesus transformed the physical matter of His body into radiation and energy.[5] This allowed the Shroud to ultimately be accepted as evidence, with no quibbling from the scientific community. Once readers have finished this book, they will be able to answer for themselves the controversial question surrounding the authenticity of Christ's shroud. The Shroud is a visual and symbolic gospel, which, needing no words in any earthly language, can be intuitively understood. Even those who are unable to read can understand its message.

The interpretation of the Shroud symbols has been taken from the previously mentioned mysticism sources, and I have summarized their meanings. The detailed descriptions I provide of the Crucifixion underscore the fact that the content of the New Revelation is mutually affirmed by the messages of the Shroud. On the more than ten thousand pages of these writings, through His innermost entreaty to a multitude people, Jesus explains His all-encompassing love, His essence, His teaching, and His creation.

Over the course of nearly thirty years of reading the writings of the mystics, I became increasingly aware of the immense importance of the Shroud, because these texts were written long before any scientific research had been conducted on the Shroud of Turin. The first photograph of the Shroud was taken in 1898, and subsequent research was undertaken in 1931. It is obvious that the mystics could not have possessed knowledge that would only be discovered much later as experts conducted research on the Shroud.

From my point of view, what Jesus is trying to do through the writings of the mystics as well as in the Shroud is to correct an error that is widespread in Christianity. In a symbol created out of His blood, He corrects the image of God that has been interpreted and handed down to us through the concept of the "Trinity," using a biblical context appropriate to our day and age. He had already foreseen this misconception during His teachings. Because of His belief in free will, Jesus lovingly accepted this interpretative latitude, just as He did His crucifixion. For Jesus, the most important prerequisite for a vibrant, trusting, and fearless Christianity is the proper understanding of His divine nature. This is why Jesus left these messages of His infinite love and His readily understandable teachings for each of us on his Shroud, so that they would reach us in our day.

God respects our free will. Because He loves us, He helps us when we call upon Him. This is why we urgently need a new vision for Christianity. If we are to have a positive influence on our collective destiny, we human beings need a renewed closer connection with His Holy Spirit,[6] the personal Comforter and Helper promised by Christ.

This is all I wish to say in advance regarding my central theses, for which this book is intended to be a detailed justification, but which, nevertheless, ultimately merely provides an outline of them. The scope of the topic is so great that it does not allow more than a general overview. Despite this, or perhaps precisely because of this, I would like to acquaint you, dear reader, with a personal insight that I consider important: To me, the "Shroud of Christ in Turin" and the "Great Gospel of

John" by Jakob Lorber are the two most valuable treasures we humans possess!

Finally, a brief note about this book. As a rule, boldface or other emphasis has been used in the quotations as a stylistic device. Texts in square brackets represent additions that we, the authors, have made to the quotes. Any emphasis that was present in the original text will be noted as such.

I hope that you will enjoy this book and the illustrations in it. It would please me greatly to hear from you. Perhaps one day we will have the opportunity to discuss any unanswered questions together.

Yours in Christ,
Gisela Elisabeth Heinz

---

1   The capitalized pronouns (I, Mine, Me His, Him, He, etc.) in the quotations from the New Revelation always refer to the Lord.

2   Lorber, Jakob: *The Great Gospel of John*. Volumes 1–10. Received through the Inner Word by Jakob Lorber. *The Detailed Account of Jesus' Time of Teaching*, Volume 9, Chapter 89, Paragraphs 9–11. For all additional quotations, I will cite the title abbreviation, the chapter, and the paragraph(s), e.g., GGJ 9, 89, 9–11.
    The quotations and excerpts have been taken from the books of the New Revelation and the translations were adapted for this book by Dr. Dyre.

3   Servants of hedonism and idolatry

4   Most of the Bible passages were taken from the King James Version.

5   Engel, Leopold: *The Great Gospel of John, Vol. 11,* Chapter 76, Paragraph 1; hereafter, GEJ 11.

6   In John's gospel, Jesus calls the Holy Spirit the "Paraclete," sent by God, whom He, Jesus Christ, will send to His disciples to encourage them in adversity, to speak for them, to help them attain their purpose. Likewise, it is the Holy Spirit who will guide them to the knowledge of God and the redeeming ministry of Jesus Christ, to repentant self-awareness and to hope (see John 14:16, 26; John 15:27; John 16:7).
    In John's first letter, Jesus Himself is described as an advocate (intercessor, helper, comforter) for us (1 John 2:1). "Paraclete" is an ancient Greek word meaning to summon, invite, comfort; the Paraclete is thus the "summoned" and the "comforter."

Foreword by the Co-Author

Dear Reader,

After more than three decades, Gisela Elisabeth Heinz has been inspired to publish her fascinating insights into the Shroud of Christ. One of the most effective guiding principles in the book also contributes to an important goal: the intention to help as many people as possible to establish a personal relationship with God by building a stable, navigable path to His Holy Spirit. For some, this will also facilitate the renewal of an earlier connection to God. The sense of peace that flows from Gisela's words shows how meaningful this intention is and how much this goal means to her. The helpful information she provides makes the Shroud messages invaluable – even groundbreaking – for those who are seeking a personal relationship with God. Gisela Heinz is a loving and exceptionally sincere person and it is a pleasure for me to be able to help her attain one of her most important life goals. Details about who I am are actually not very important. But, it was Gisela's wish to name me as co-author of her book.

I am Peter Kutzki, a friend and confidant of the author, and for some time now, the man of her heart. I would simply like to take this opportunity to explain that the thoughts and ideas I have introduced in this book are intended to contribute to an understanding of a sometimes difficult spiritual quest. From my very first reading of a draft of this book, I felt that the topics listed in the Contents were presented within a harmoniously coherent manuscript. I believe my positive feelings were also inspired by the way in which the well-balanced level-headedness of the Shroud resonated within me. Gisela shared important details of her Shroud findings with me, and, with this in mind, I was able to help refine individual sections of her manuscript. We worked together on most of the chapters, aiming to make them as clear as possible. However, there was no way for me, in the space of just a few months, to attain Gisela's level of knowledge, gained from more than thirty years of studying the Shroud, along with the more than ten thousand pages of the New Revelation she had read. During the course of our work together, however, I was soon able to understand the meaning and the sequence of thoughts that would provide structure for our shared work. For instance, to be able to understand these writings and to also grasp them in context, knowledge of the relationship between the Shroud of Christ and the New Revelation is essential. This is one of the elements that helps to illustrate and illuminate why, over the centuries, some very tragic misunderstandings have been caused by misrepresentation of and carelessly confusing references to the Trinity of God. I carefully studied the texts of the mystical prophecies of Jakob Lorber and Gottfried Mayerhofer. Many of the utterances, received from God, proclaim that He, Jesus Christ, and the Holy Spirit are to be understood as being united in a single entity as God, the Father. The alternating comparison between the Shroud of Christ and the New Revelation serves to illustrate and reinforce the divine messages involved. At their core and in combination, the symbols of the Shroud are easily recognizable, and the messages of The New Revelation are unambiguous.

In a later chapter, I will share my personal insights on this topic with you. I came to my conclusions by relating my own thoughts and memories to the very interesting information contained in this book. One of the things that fascinated me most during the course of our work together was the ongoing growth I experienced and the impact it has had and continues to have on me, still to this day. I am convinced of the truth of the New Revelation and the resulting significance of the messages of Christ's shroud for our times.

And so, dear reader, I wish you much joy and success in your search for the Miraculous! Perhaps you will allow one or another of the illustrations of the Shroud of Turin to guide you? In any event, I wish you much pleasure in reading this book and hope that it will provide you with many valuable insights.

Yours in Christ, Peter Kutzki

"Faith and knowledge are as the two scales of a balance;
as one rises, the other falls."
Arthur Schopenhauer

Introduction

The purpose of this book can be illustrated with a line from a German children's prayer, the English translation of which is:

> "The grace of God and Jesus' blood make all that would harm us into good."

The authors' objective is to explain the messages that Jesus Christ left for us on His shroud, which, with the help of more recent mysticism, each of us can personally recognize and understand. Examples of occurrences over the centuries when Jesus Christ has appeared directly, along with immersion into the world of images from early Christian art found in Ravenna, Italy, will help readers to deepen and strengthen a trusting relationship with our Creator and to use it to attain their own personal salvation.

In Jesus, God was manifested visibly and tangibly for all of His creatures and for all eternity as the "Son of Man." Following His resurrection and ascension to heaven, Jesus became the FATHER-GOD, who can be perceived by all of His creatures. His essence is love, infused with wisdom and power. There are not three different forms of God! The Trinity, as it is taught and portrayed, is a reinterpretation of the old term "persona." This term comes from the Latin *personare* (literally, a "sounding-through") and denotes the blending of different characteristics, but not of individual persons.

Perhaps it will be a little easier for our human comprehension to grasp this if, for the sake of comparison, we think about the three-dimensional quality of everything that is part of our daily experience. A house, a tree, or a mountain – all have three dimensions: length, width, and height. And no one would say that this means that there are really three houses, three trees, or three mountains. God wants us to understand his "folded-into-three" being as a single entity, not as three separate Gods. God is a being with three special and indivisible qualities. An analogous image would be that of a flame, which radiates light and heat. God is absolute Love (the Father). This Love radiates Wisdom (the Son) and Power (the Holy Spirit).

The humans of this world are the "children of God" and the "crown of creation." As the "crown of creation," we are the ultimate result and endpoint of the evolution of physical creatures. Death is the beginning of spiritual life. Jesus wants to reveal Himself personally to each of His children who long for Him. Teachers (clergy) can be very helpful in this, but they are not absolutely necessary for establishing contact between the FATHER and the child.

Many converts have experienced a first-hand encounter with Jesus Christ. Examples of this include the apostle Paul, the seer Emanuel Swedenborg, and the wandering monk from India, Sadhu Sundar Singh, all of whom I will discuss in more detail later in this book.

Those who have been directly converted by Jesus consistently reject the customary psychological explanations for this event and strongly assert the supernatural presence of grace that they have experienced. Their testimonies reveal that these transformations are nothing like traditional conversions. Virtually all of these believers affirm that they have experienced the direct intervention of pure divine power, and thus Christ. Everyone who has been personally touched by Jesus will tell you that this was not a human experience or some inner spiritual event, but a revelation of the divine reality. All those who have experienced this inner transformation, but cannot describe it and yet still wish to testify to the overwhelming sensation, describe a wonderfully peaceful feeling.

Encounters with Christ

The Apostle Paul

The New Testament (NT) tells the story of the transformation of Saul of Tarsus, who later renamed himself Paul, as he traveled the road to Damascus. On his journey to persecute the Christians of Damascus, he encounters the resurrected Jesus. Paul himself recounts this in Acts 22:6-16:

> Repentance: Called by Christ
> [6]And it came to pass, that, as I made my journey, and was come nigh unto Damascus about noon, suddenly there shone from heaven a great light round about me. [7]And I fell unto the ground, and heard a voice saying unto me, "Saul, Saul, why persecutest thou me?" [8]And I answered, "Who art thou, Lord?" And he said unto me, "I am Jesus of Nazareth, whom thou persecutes." [9]And they that were with me saw indeed the light, and were afraid; but they heard not the voice of him that spake to me. [10]And I said, "What shall I do, Lord?" And the Lord said unto me, "Arise, and go into Damascus; and there it shall be told thee of all things which are appointed for thee to do." [11]And when I could not see for the glory of that light, being led by the hand of them that were with me, I came into Damascus.
> [12]And one Ananias, a devout man according to the law, having a good report of all the Jews which dwelt there, [13]came unto me, and stood, and said unto me, "Brother Saul, receive thy sight." And the same hour I looked up upon him. [14]And he said, "The God of our fathers hath chosen thee, that thou shouldest know his will, and see that Just One, and shouldest hear the voice of his mouth. [15]For thou shalt be his witness unto all men of what thou hast seen and heard. [16]And now why tarriest thou? Arise, and be baptized, and wash away thy sins, calling on the name of the Lord."

Following this decisive event, Jesus commissions Paul to becomes an apostle to the nations.

Emanuel Swedenborg

A remorseful Swedenborg encountered Jesus Christ as he was undergoing a crisis of meaning in his life. But, let us allow Swedenborg to speak for himself about the vision that led to his calling:

I observed that the following words were placed in my mouth: "O most almighty Jesus Christ, who in Your great mercy deigns to come to such a sinner, make me worthy of Your grace!" I lifted up my hands and was praying when a hand came and forcefully pressed my hands. I then continued the prayer: "O You who promised to accept all sinners by Your grace, You can do no other than to keep Your word!" Then I lay upon His breast and beheld Him face to face. It was a face so full of holiness that I cannot describe it. He smiled, and I truly believe that His face had been so during His life on earth. He turned to me and asked if I had a "testament of health."

Swedenborg made his first trip to England as a young man, entering the country illegally, yet without incident, even though he was traveling from a country where the plague was raging. He snuck into the "promised land" of scientific knowledge and nearly paid for this on the gallows. He thereafter viewed himself as having left the land of selfishness, scholarly vanity, and natural knowledge, and, after crossing the sea of doubt, temptations, and purification, having landed on the shores of essence and truth.

I replied, "O Lord, You know this better than I," to which He said, "Do this, therefore!" This means, as I understood it in my heart: "truly love me" or "do what you have promised!" O God, grant me mercy for this! I understood that I could not do this through my own strength. I sensed an inner joy that filled my entire being.[1]

Jesus' question was a test for Swedenborg, to determine whether he was worthy to enter into the sacred realm. This experience shook Swedenborg profoundly and marked a decisive turning point in his life.

Sadhu Sundar Singh

THE REVELATION OF THE LIVING CHRIST
According to the views I had at that time, I thought that by burning the Gospel I had done a good deed. But the restlessness in my heart grew, and afterwards I felt very miserable for two days. On the third day, when I felt that I could not bear it any longer, I got up at three o'clock in the morning, took my bath and prayed: if there be any God at all, let Him reveal himself to me, show me the way of salvation, and put an end to this unrest in my soul. I was determined that if this prayer remained without an answer, I would go down to the

railroad tracks before daybreak and lay my head on the rails in front of the in-coming train. I remained in prayer until about half past three in the morning and expected to see Krishna or Buddha or some other Hindu divinity. None appeared, but a light suddenly shone in the room. I opened the door to see where it came from, but outside, it was dark. I went back inside and the light grew stronger and stronger until it took the shape of a cloud of light hovering over the floor. In this light appeared not the shape I was expecting, but – the Living Christ, whom I had thought to be dead. Until the end of time, I will never forget His glorious and loving face, nor the few words He said: "Why do you persecute Me? Behold, I died on the cross for you and for the whole world." As if by a lightning strike, these words were burned into my heart, and I fell to the ground before Him. My heart was filled with unspeakable joy and peace, and my entire life would be completely transformed. At that moment, the old Sundar Singh died, and a new Sundar Singh was born, whose purpose was to serve the Living Christ.[2]

1   Gollwitzer, Gerhard: *Die Durchsichtige Welt. Ein Swedenborg Brevier*, p. 16. Translated by C. Dyre
2   Die Offenbarung, Sadhu Sundar Singh (1888–1929) penultimate section. Published at: www.jesus-der-christus.info/zgsingh.htm, [accessed on September 26, 2018]. Translation by C. Dyre.

Prophets, Mystics and the New Revelation

The writings contained in the Bible are an attempt to establish and pre-serve a personal relationship between God and man. Often, our tradi-tions stray from the original intent of the divine messages. The divine source therefore has its "own plans." So it is, that time and again, pro-nouncements have been made by some very wise individuals. Often, these proclamations of the divine will have been subjected to non-objec-tive debate and criticism.

> [12]I have yet many things to say unto you, but ye cannot bear them now. [13]Howbeit when he, the Spirit of truth, is come, he will guide you into all truth: for he shall not speak of himself; but whatsoever he shall hear, that shall he speak: and he will shew you things to come. [14]He shall glorify me: for he shall receive of mine, and shall shew it unto you. [15]All things that the Father hath are mine: therefore said I, that he shall take of mine, and shall shew it unto you. [John 16:12–15]

Here, Jesus describes the task that will be taken on by future prophets, who will speak to us in His name to teach us what, in our times and beyond the Gospels, is needed for our salvation. In the German-speaking countries, part of this pronouncement was fulfilled in the second half of the nine-teenth century, with the New Revelation writings of the German mystics.

It was in these that Gottfried Mayerhofer, Jakob Lorber and others, inspired by the Holy Spirit, provided us with the information we need to more perfectly understand Christianity. This includes the "The Lord's Sermons" for each Sunday of the year, with a spiritual interpretation of the nineteenth-century Catholic Gospel texts (Mayerhofer), a compre-hensive explanation of Jesus' teachings, a much more detailed descrip-tion of the events of His life, and revelations about the earth and the uni-verse. These texts were of great help to me in understanding the symbols on the Shroud of Christ.

To help make the messages of the mystics included in this book easier to understand, I would like to first address the following question: "What exactly is Christian mysticism?" The term "mysticism" comes from the ancient Greek word *mystiko*, meaning "mysterious," and gener-ally refers to spiritual experiences that cannot be otherwise explained.

In essence, Christian mysticism is a phenomenon that is nearly impossible to put into words. Mystics tell us that to be able to speak about mysticism and to fully comprehend it, it is necessary to have first experienced it yourself. For anyone who has not had this experience, however, mysticism can only be indirectly described through reference to its manifestations. True understanding, however, is only possible through personal experience.

It is easy for us to understand that anyone who has never been in love before will not be able to understand the phenomenon of being in love. We can only understand what people in love actually feel once we have experienced it for ourselves. One typical phenomenon in mysticism is "divine knowledge." However, the predominant phenomenon experienced by mystics is the "love from and for God." Love of God is the true driving force behind mysticism. Likewise, for all Christian believers, it is the unique love they experience from and for Jesus that flows into and out of the core of their souls. As mentioned in the foreword, there is no other way for human free will to develop in a way that is unconstrained and unconditional. In this light, we should not be blaming God so much for the state of today's world, but rather consider it the effect of the free will of all people.

As will be discussed in the chapters written by my co-author, Peter, I, too, was encouraged by the opinions and world views expressed by renowned scientists who have made outstanding contributions to modern physics. First and foremost among these are the recipients of the Nobel Prize for Physics: Max Planck, Albert Einstein, and Werner Heisenberg.

In the following sections, I will present four Christian visionaries. The mystics Emanuel Swedenborg, Jakob Lorber, Gottfried Mayerhofer and Leopold Engel all vividly describe the divine inspiration that overcame them as they explain how and what they experienced and felt as the divine messages were given them. The language and expressions they use may seem a bit foreign and outdated to today's reader, but they reflect the language commonly used in their lifetimes.

Figure 1: Emanuel Swedenborg[2]

Emanuel Swedenborg

Swedenborg was born on January 28, 1688, the son of a Swedish preacher who would later go on to become a Bishop.[1] After completing his studies, he traveled to England in 1710, where at that time, scientific researchers were making groundbreaking discoveries. At the height of his renown as a scientist, he fell into a deep religious crisis. This continued for eight years, until he was finally permitted to experience Jesus.

The year following Swedenborg's experience of the appearance of Jesus was an eventful one. It concluded in London, with the vision that led to his calling. On an April night in 1745, the Lord appeared to Swedenborg and told him that he had chosen him to explain the true spiritual meaning of the Bible to the world. The Lord himself would dictate what he should write. From that day on, in accordance with the Lord's instructions, Swedenborg renounced all secular study and, for the next 27 years of his life, devoted himself solely to spiritual matters.

At first, Swedenborg provided descriptions of the spiritual realm. Later, he progressed to a systematic description of "The Doctrine of the Lord for the New Church." For all questions posed in the "The Doctrine of the Lord for the New Church," he explicitly references the writings contained in the Holy Scriptures, which he pronounces anew to be supremely sacred and the "fullness" of divine revelation.

As spiritual persons, humans have the freedom to live out the life breathed into them by God in their own individual ways. They are therefore not slaves, but free partners with God, from whom God hopes for loving devotion. In this freedom lies the dignity of the relationship between God and man.

In creating human beings to whom he granted free will, God created a counterpart for Himself, one whom He loves and whose love He seeks.

God and man are thereby mutually dependent upon each other, they need one another.

A major misconception that is found primarily in the churches of the western world is the erroneous doctrine of the triune nature of God. "This irrational doctrine is responsible for the emergence of naturalism and atheism." In his work "True Christianity," Swedenborg explains further what he means: "Father, Son, and Holy Spirit are three manifestations of the one God, and their unity is to be understood such as the unity of soul, body, and actions, all three, in one man."

Even in the earliest days of the Church, falsehoods were already permeating and corrupting the new truths of illumination. This is why God has been compelled to intervene over and over again, by granting new revelations. In a letter to the prelate Oettinger, Swedenborg prophesied the coming of a seer who would receive much more through inner divination than he himself had. This prophecy can be understood to point to Jakob Lorber.

Johann Wolfgang von Goethe also adopted much of Swedenborg's thinking. By the age of twenty, he was already studying Swedenborg's spiritual writings and his religious evolution was strongly influenced by Swedenborg. His *Faust*, the most well-known of all German dramas, is –notably, at the beginning and in the second part – heavily inspired by Swedenborg's writings. However, because Goethe's biographers were generally not well-acquainted with Swedenborg, there has not yet been any sufficiently in-depth examination of this relationship.

Jakob Lorber – A True Prophet?

Lorber was born on July 22, 1800 in Kanischa, Austria. In 1817, he began his education in Marburg, studying to become a primary school teacher, and from 1824 to 1829, he worked as a private tutor in Graz. Beginning in 1830, he earned his living by teaching singing, piano, and violin as well as through concert performances. Lorber also composed a number of his own works, which led to his acquaintance with the composer Anselm Huettenbrenner. On March 15, 1840, following his calling to be the "Scribe of God," and through inner divination, he began to write his first work, "The Household of God."

Figure: 2: Jakob Lorber[3]

From that time on, he chose to renounce the idea of any professional career and instead earned his living as a private music teacher. His first priority was to write down his revelations, which ultimately amounted to some 25 volumes. In a letter to a friend, Jakob Lorber wrote on February 16, 1858:

With regard to the inner word, as one hears it, I can only say, speaking of myself, that I always hear the Lord's most holy word in the region of the heart like a most clear thought, light and pure, like pronounced words. No one, no matter how close he may be, can hear anything from any voice, but for me this voice of grace sounds brighter than any loud material sound. But that is all I can tell you from my experience. (GGJ 1, p. 8)

The word "prophet" comes from the Greek and means "herald." Jakob Lorber was therefore a herald for God's messages. We may ask ourselves today if these were truly authentic messages from God. When we hear something proclaimed to us, we are able to accept it as true if it aligns with our knowledge and experience or to reject it as false if we know the facts to be different.

During Lorber's life and creative period, his friends and patrons did not have the benefit of the knowledge that we have today. Today, almost 180 years later, it is much easier for us, as people seeking substantiation, to believe his revelations.

In my judgement, we now have ample evidence that confirms Lorber as a true mystic. In my experience, he is the only Christian prophet who, among his revelations, also described natural scientific knowledge that would only be discovered and proven in the far distant future. Lorber died on August 24, 1864 in Graz.

Lorber's Scientific Prophecies[4]

A prophet who is led to reveal natural scientific insights that will only be confirmed by science decades later may also find the validity of his spiritual and intellectual revelations called into question. For believers seeking God, Lorber's religious revelations may seem more important than his scientific predictions. However, for people who today are searching for a convincing rationale, Lorber's scientific prophecies are no less fascinating. Along with the revelation in which he states that all matter is in fact truly spirit, Lorber was also led to describe the character of light long before the particle nature and wave-like characteristics of light would be discovered. He also described the structure of an atom: the turbulently rapid movement within the atom and the swift oscillation of the protons, which oscillate at rate of one hundred trillion times per second. When Lorber described the image of the electrons racing around the atomic nucleus as a haze, this term comes very close to the modern description. Atomic physicists refer to these as electron clouds.

Lorber also correctly identified the lifespan of the absolute smallest of the elementary particles at one trillionth of a second. Scientists have been able to confirm this for the eta meson and the sigma baryon particles.

What was true for the microcosm, in this case, the atom, would also prove to be true for the macrocosm, namely, the universe. Long before scientists discovered the existence of additional galaxy systems in the cosmos, Lorber was able to describe the structure of the universe with its galaxies, solar systems, and planetary systems. The planet Neptune was discovered just four years after Lorber described it. It took nearly a century longer for astronomers to discover the "super suns," quasars, whose brightness is billions of times stronger than that of our sun.

When Lorber announced the existence of solar universes or "universes of solar universes," as he called them, with a million times greater luminosity than our sun, it was impossible for people to fathom. Modern research, however, provides us with these examples: the quasar 3C 273 has the energy of 1000 large galaxies, each with 100 billion suns, and CTA 102 has a hundred trillion times more energy than our sun.

These descriptions of Lorber's must have sounded like the ravings of a lunatic to his contemporaries. Who could possibly imagine something a billion times more brilliant than our sun? It was only with the deployment of space probes that we also learned conclusively that moons always turn toward their planets from the same side or that the Earth is in fact pear-shaped. These modern findings, made possible only through space exploration, were, however, also anticipated by Lorber.

Gottfried Mayerhofer

Figure 3: Gottfried Meyerhofer[5]

In a letter to Johannes Busch in Dresden, dated August 28, 1870, Mayerhofer wrote:

In His grace, the Lord often gives me only that which is not fully comprehensible to my friends here, and which is to be used – who knows when and by whom – in a regulated sequence for successive instruction. And thus, it often happens that there are dictations in which nothing new is expressed, but only recitations of things that have been told before in another form; I am always quite passive in such communications, very seldom knowing with what they are concerned. Usually, I am beset by an inexplicable restlessness, and am compelled to then sit at my desk. Only when I take the pencil in my hand do I learn *what the Lord wants*, and even then, I know neither the beginning nor the sequence nor the end; indeed, not one word sooner than the other. – So, for example, it [His Word] says to me: Take the Gospel of John, Chapter 3, verse 7, etc. I am not at all well-acquainted with the Bible, so I know nothing of the content of the chapter or verse, and I seek it out, sit down, and write what is dictated to me. – My dictations are thus created, through no will of my own and without knowledge of why or for what reason, in this way and not in any other [emphasis in the original.][6]

Born in November 1807, Mayerhofer was the son of a Bavarian officer. He studied mathematics, later becoming a lecturer on the subject, before embarking on a military career that took him to Greece. In 1833, he married Aspasia von Isay, the daughter of an Athenian merchant. Around 1837, at the request of his wife, Mayerhofer made the decision to retire from his military post and move with her to Trieste, along with his father-in-law.

He remained there until his death. Mayerhofer was financially dependent on his wife's family fortune. During his extended retirement, he devoted himself to music, landscape painting and spiritual matters.

Mayerhofer read the writings of Jakob Lorber, with which he had become acquainted through his friendship with a Dr. Waidele, a military physician from Graz. In Graz, Waidele had belonged to the inner circle surrounding Lorber and, because the books were not easily obtainable at that time, in Trieste he continued to eagerly copy out Lorber's texts by hand. The deeper Mayerhofer delved into the writings of this Styrian mystic, also copying them by hand himself, the more enthusiastic he became.

In March 1870, he heard the "voice of the Lord" speak within him. For the next seven years, leading up to his death in 1877, Mayerhofer dedicated himself, in a manner similar to his role model, Lorber, to his work as a visionary and writer. Christoph Friedrich Landbeck (1840–1921), his friend and, to some extent, also his student, described the writing process in roughly these words: Before Mayerhofer would begin to write something down, that morning, he would see, in his mind's eye, clear images of the objects to be addressed. As he proceeded to write, however, the vividness of the visions would often become blurred, resulting in some stylistic imperfections. Mayerhofer once wrote that the Lord only gave him information that would be comprehensible to his friends and which could perhaps be used for a series of lessons. He was always very passive during these communications and very rarely had any idea what they were about. Generally, he would be overcome with an inexplicable restlessness, prompting him to sit down at his desk, and only once he had picked up a pencil would he know what the Lord wanted him to write, though he would not know how it would begin, what the sequence would be, or how it would end, and he was not given one word earlier than the next.

To protect his ailing eyes, Mayerhofer sometimes dictated what he heard to his student, Christoph Landbeck. He was also able to discern the spiritual being behind the physical human shell and had the ability to heal.

Figure 4: Leopold Engel[7]

Leopold Engel

Biographical Information

Leopold Engel lived from 1858 to 1931. His father, Karl Dietrich Engel (1824–1913), an excellent musician and violin virtuoso, had been engaged in 1846 as the concertmaster in the Russian State Theater Orchestra in St. Petersburg. Upon his retirement, the family moved back to Germany, living in Berlin, Bremen, Oldenburg, and Dresden, where Leopold attended school. Around 1886, Engel began his work as a writer. Between 1891 and 1893, he wrote the eleventh volume of the Great Gospel of John, the texts of which had been given Engel as a spiritual dictation from God.

At a very early age, as an eleven-year-old boy, Engel's father introduced him to the works of Jakob Lorber. Later, he also made the acquaintance of Johannes Busch, the first publisher of the Lorber writings, in Dresden. However, at no time did the thought occur to him that he himself might be called to become a scribe. Although he grew up in a religious family, he was not much different from other boys his age. He enjoyed an excellent education in Dresden, where he took a particular interest in the natural sciences. His inner convictions developed independently, with no pressure from his father, and there were also periods during which his faith wavered and he became occupied with worldly things. In the depths of his heart, however, was an inner sanctum, which he kept hidden, so that it could not be defiled by deniers and scoffers: this was and is his unconditional belief in the essence of God as revealed in Christ.

When he was twenty-two, Engel began a stage career and achieved not inconsiderable success as an actor in a number of different theaters. In the long run, however, he found his career in the theater unsatisfying, and began to search for a job that would not require him to constantly move from place to place. Following several futile attempts, he ultimately returned to the theater. In 1889, he was finally able to turn his back on his acting career, and from then on, made a modest living as a writer. His call to the task of writing down the Great Gospel of John came in 1891, which he recounts as follows:

I had made an agreement with a friend of mine, a kindred spirit, to help him in his business ventures and to expand upon and possibly enhance an invention he had been working on. I therefore went to Leipzig and lodged with this friend. After some time, the persistent and increasingly intense thought pursued me, that I would be able to write the conclusion to Lorber's works on John. I dismissed this thought; it seemed to me both fanciful and false. Why should I, of all people, be granted this grace? I did not feel myself worthy of it at all. But the internal pressure increased daily, becoming unbearable, and I told my friend of the experience, and also of my reasoned opinion, that only falsehoods would be revealed. My friend shook his head and said dryly: "If I were you, I would simply calmly sit down and begin writing. If it is complete nonsense, we shall see it for what it is and toss it in the rubbish." In short, he gave me encouragement, and I followed his advice (GGJ 11, P. 6)[8]

And, his explanation of the inner voice:

I am often asked how the inner voice expresses itself, and I can only answer as follows: In my writings, I distinguish between precisely three different types. First, there are the words that originate from me, myself, as a product of my own knowledge or imagination. When I read through such a text later, even if many years have passed, I always recognize what I have written as the result of my work. As I read it, it will not seem strange to me. The second type is one of simple inspiration, a transmission of thoughts from distant spheres. Here, it is not words, but thoughts, that flow to me, which I must cloak in words myself. Half of the result of this process would seem to be mine – in essence, however, it is not; for without this transference of thoughts, I would not be able to create anything of value. The mood, tranquility, and neutrality of my inner being all contribute to success. Any disturbance interrupts the work immediately, and then it is not very difficult for one's own thoughts to sneak in, and, if the imagination is vivid, even to corrupt the inspiration completely. Caution and self-critique are urgently necessary at this stage, for it is here that derisive spirits like to do their mischief, and nonsense can easily become a technique. Later, when reading what has been written, it often seems strange; one wonders then whether he has ever written it, although he remembers one thing or another more or less clearly. The third and final type is often a mystery to one's own mind. The compulsion already described may arise, but then, upon request, the clear perception of an inner speaker may also emerge, much in the same way as when you recall a conversation with a friend, it seems that you are hearing him speak. A dialogue ensues. Questions and answers, clear explanations of matters that one did not know about before and which – this is a characteristic sign –, if they are not captured in writing, easily vanish from one's memory. The latter is evidence of authenticity, because one will remember anything that comes from one's own thoughts. During this and the previous type of writing, the sense of the hand being guided often serves as a sign to the scribe that an external force is at work. What has been written down vanishes so quickly from the writer's memory that he must first read through the text thoroughly in order to absorb the contents. After some time has passed, genuinely manifested texts will always appear to him as having not been written down by him. Should this not be the case, then I would assume at least some intermingling with his own thought, that is, the second type of writing, but with greater clarity. Only keen self-criticism and the highest degree of neutrality can lead to manifestations of the true inner word. (GGJ) 11, p. 7.[9]

The results of Engel's work can be found in the final volume of the New Revelation.

1   *EMANUEL SWEDENBORG und seine geistige Ausstrahlung.* Biographical excerpts, pp. 1–20.

2   Emanuel Swedenborg, detail of painting by Carl Frederik von Breda, public domain, https://de.wikipedia.org/wiki/Emanuel_Swedenborg

3   Jakob Lorber; public domain, Neu Salems Verlag – Briefe Lorbers (Lorber's Letters) (1931). https://de.wikipedia.org/wiki/Jakob_Lorber

4   Kurt Eggenstein has written a brief and clear overview of these revelations in his booklet *Der unbekannte Prophet Jakob Lorber (The Unkown Prophet Jakob Lorber)*, pp 14–43. An English translation of portions of the book may be found at: http://www.akademijavjecnogproljeca.org/lorber/eng/lorber_proof_eggen. html (accessed Sept. 8, 2020).

5   Gottfried Mayerhofer, public domain, unknown. https://de.wikipedia.org/wiki/ Gottfried_Mayerhofer#/media/Datei:Mayerhofer.jpg (accessed Sept. 8, 2020)

6   Mayerhofer, Gottfried: *Predigten des Herrn (The Lord's Sermons)*, p. 6. English translation by C. Dyre.

7   Leopold Engel, public domain, unknown artist. https://de.wikipedia.org/wiki/ Leopold_Engel

8   Translation by C. Dyre

9   Translation by C. Dyre

The Shroud of Christ

Throughout the year, a replica of the Shroud of Turin (Figure 5[1]) is on exhibit in the Cathedral of Turin. The original Shroud itself is displayed every 25 years or so. In 1998, a special exhibition of the Shroud was mounted in memory of Secondo Pia, who, in 1898, was the first to photograph the Shroud. From the very first day the Shroud was exhibited in Turin, an endless stream of Christians has flocked to the city to view it. If this piece of cloth is indeed the shroud in which the body of Christ was buried and out of which he rose, it is the most important relic in the history of Christianity.

Figure 5: Shroud of Turin

No other object in our culture has provoked such a violent clash of theories and counterarguments as the Shroud. All of the significant scientific disciplines have attempted to address the subject and there is no shortage of wildly speculative efforts to explain the illustrations on the Shroud.

In the meantime, however, scientists have declared the Shroud of Turin to be a genuine photographic "negative" of the front and back of a crucified man who bears all of the wounds described in the Gospels as those inflicted upon Jesus Christ. This "negative" also reveals spatial information about the body it depicts. The Italian Academy of Sciences (ENEA) has declared the image on the cloth to be of supernatural origin.

The Historical Account of the Shroud of Christ

The official history of the existence of the Shroud in the western world begins between 1353 and 1356, when it was first exhibited in Lirey, a small county in France, southeast of Paris. From that time on, its history has been fully tracked, up to the present day.

Although the Gospels contain references to the Shroud of Christ, all mention of it disappears following Christ's resurrection. It vanishes into the darkness of history during the early centuries and not until the sixth century does it re-emerge, in Edessa, the present-day Sanli Urfa in eastern Turkey. According to the writings of Lorber in his Abgarus letter, Jesus decided that immediately following His death, His shroud would be brought to Edessa. This is also supported by the "Abgar legend," dating from the fourth to the sixth century, which has been handed down in a variety of versions. Edessa is the site where the Shroud was folded so that only the face of the crucified man could be seen, leading to it also being referred to as the "Tetradiplon," the Greek word for a cloth that is "four-double-folded."

Some coins, such as the ninth-century coin of Basil I, show that the full length of the Shroud was already known at that time. In the depiction, the right foot appears to be twisted. On the Shroud, the right leg, which is crossed over the left, seems to be shorter. The artists of the first millennium did not employ perspectival foreshortening, but deliberately chose to use the "reverse perspective" to allude to the transcendence out of reality and convey the sense of "not-made-by-human-hands."[2] On Orthodox crosses, therefore, the right foot is shorter than the left and the suppedaneum (small platform attached to the cross to support the feet of the person being crucified) is not horizontal, but at an angle.

During the tenth century, the emperor Romanus Lakapensos sought to bring the Shroud to Constantinople. He therefore besieged the city of Edessa until the Shroud was handed over to him. Once in Constantinople, it was preserved and exhibited in the Pharos Chapel. In his famous sermon of August 15, 944, on the occasion of the transfer of the Shroud to Constantinople, Gregory Referendarius, Archdeacon of Hagia Sophia, declared in a detailed description of the Shroud that "one could see where the blood had spurted from the side of the body." This sermon has been handed down in a version from the eleventh century and is preserved in the Vatican. Gregory did not believe the cloth to be a shroud, but instead was of the opinion, supported by tradition, that it was actually an image of the living Christ, still stained with blood from the wound in His side. The sermon also includes further descriptions of King Abgar's conversation with the apostle Thaddaeus, who brought the cloth to Edessa, about the miraculous power of the cloth:

> You have taught me correctly about how Christ came down to earth, about his amazing miracles and his suffering, about his burial and resurrection, and about how he was miraculously taken up to the Father in his body, and I confess that he is the true God. But tell me how the image on the linen that cured me was made, since I can see it was not produced with ordinary paint, and explain its special strength, since when I saw it unfolded on your face [Thaddeus had presumably unfolded the cloth over his body to show it] I was cured of my illness and got up from my bed, and I felt the strength that I had in my body when I was in my prime.[3]

Thaddeus then explained to him that the extraordinary power of the Shroud resided in the person who had created it.

Medieval representations of the dead Christ, in which His upper body protrudes from the tomb and His hands are crossed over His torso, are also related to the Shroud of Turin. These representations are referred to as the "Imago Pietatis" or "Man of Sorrows." Perhaps these icons were a reaction of the Eastern Orthodox Church to the loss of the Shroud during the conquest of Constantinople.

The Pharus Chapel housed a wooden structure that was used on festive occasions to lift the nearly one-thousand-year-old Shroud of Christ out of the case in which it was kept and display it to the faithful. Within the folds of the Shroud, traces of the wood used for this mechanism were found.

During the conquest of Constantinople by the Venetians in 1204, the Shroud disappeared from the city and would not resurface again until between 1353 and 1356 in Lirey, France. There are numerous theories as to how the Shroud made its way to France. It may have been in the possession of the Templars, almost all of whom were later tortured and burned alive for worshipping the face of a bearded man. The Shroud's first documented owner in France was Geoffroy de Charny, a standard-

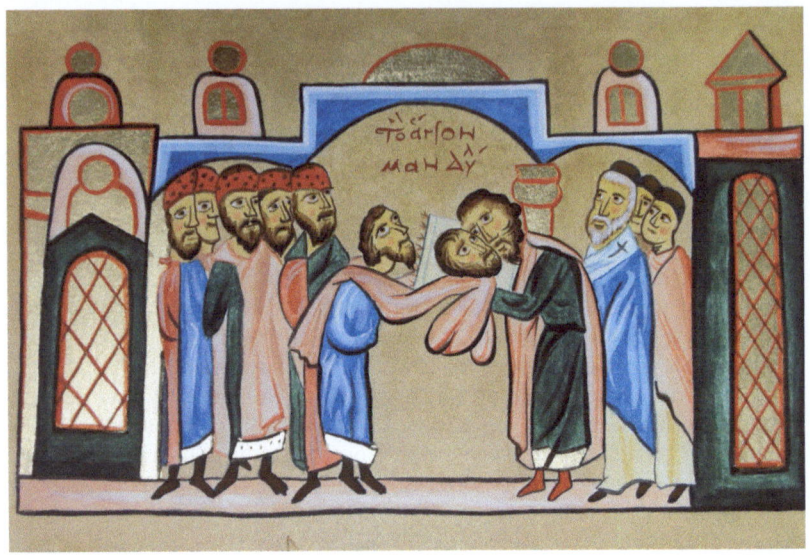

Figure 6: *Reproduction by Kirsten Voss of "The Surrender of the Mandylion to the Byzantines in 944" from the illustrated manuscript of the Madrid Skylitz. www.welt-der-ikonen.de*

bearer and crusader who never revealed how he came into possession of the Shroud.

In 1453, the Shroud came into the possession of the Dukes of Savoy and was kept in a chapel in Chambéry, where it nearly fell victim to a fire in 1532. The damage caused by the fire was mended with golden needles by nuns at the convent of the Poor Clares, who knelt on the floor in devotion as they completed this sacred task.

In 1578, Duke Emmanuel Filibert of Savoy had the Shroud transferred from Chambéry to Turin, where it has been housed in the cathedral ever since. The last King of Italy, Umberto II, bequeathed the Shroud to Pope John Paul II and the Vatican in 1983, but it remained housed in Turin. On April 12, 1997, the Shroud almost fell victim again to yet another fire, but thanks to the heroic efforts of Italian fireman Mario Trematore, it was saved from destruction.

The Influence of the Shroud on Christian Art to the Present Day

The first pictorial representations of Jesus are those of the Good Shepherd. The cross was used only as a symbol. Later, the iconographic figure of the Pantocrator, the Ruler of All and Creator of the World, appeared. A good example of this is the well-known sixth-century icon in St. Catherine's Monastery on Mount Sinai, where the features of the Shroud are clearly depicted on the face of Christ. In the Romanesque period, Christ was portrayed on the cross as a divine ruler with a crown – alive and upright. It was only during the Gothic period that the depiction of Christ as suffering or dead on the cross became established: prior to 1200, this portrayal of martyrdom was rare. With the passage of time, western artists then increasingly distanced themselves from the old, Orthodox portrayals of Christ. Unfortunately, modern-day western representations are often derived entirely from the artist's imagination.

Only Orthodoxy, with its time-honored and precise reproductions of the icons, has preserved to this day the true face of Christ in its art. The Mandylion icons, as they are called, depict the existence of the Shroud of Turin in a tradition that has been uninterrupted for centuries, ever since the times in which the Shroud was created. An exhaustive art-historical study would exceed the scope of this book. However, viewed across epochs and religions, art provides a deep, soul-touching glimpse into the commonalities and roots of our Christian traditions, religion, and mysticism.

Scientific Research Since 1898

When a photograph is taken of the face on the Shroud of Turin, if we look at the photographic negative, the face appears as it does in Fig. 8. This is how the photographer Secondo Pia first observed it on May 28, 1898, more than 100 years ago. On that night, after almost 1,900 years, the symbolic message of the Shroud of Turin was revealed to a human being for the first time: the figure of Jesus Christ and His face, bearing the marks of His suffering. The Shroud is the equivalent of a negative image, which then appears on the photographic negative as a positive image, as we are accustomed to seeing it. In what follows and through to

Figure 7: The most well-known Mandylion icon, Russia, 12th-century[4]

the end of this chapter, with the kind permission of the author, Maria Grazia Siliato, I will quote excerpts from her book *Und das Grabtuch ist doch echt (And, the Shroud Is Indeed Genuine):*[5]

On May 28, 1898, Secondo Pia, an attorney and councilman from Turin, who was also a well-respected amateur photographer, was invited to be the first photographer in history to capture the image of the Shroud of Turin. Neither he nor anyone else could suspect that a sensational event was about to unfold. The image proved almost impossible to capture photographically, but Pia refused to give up. Stubborn as he was, he corrected his work several times and then, on that mild evening of May 28, using large photo plates measuring 50

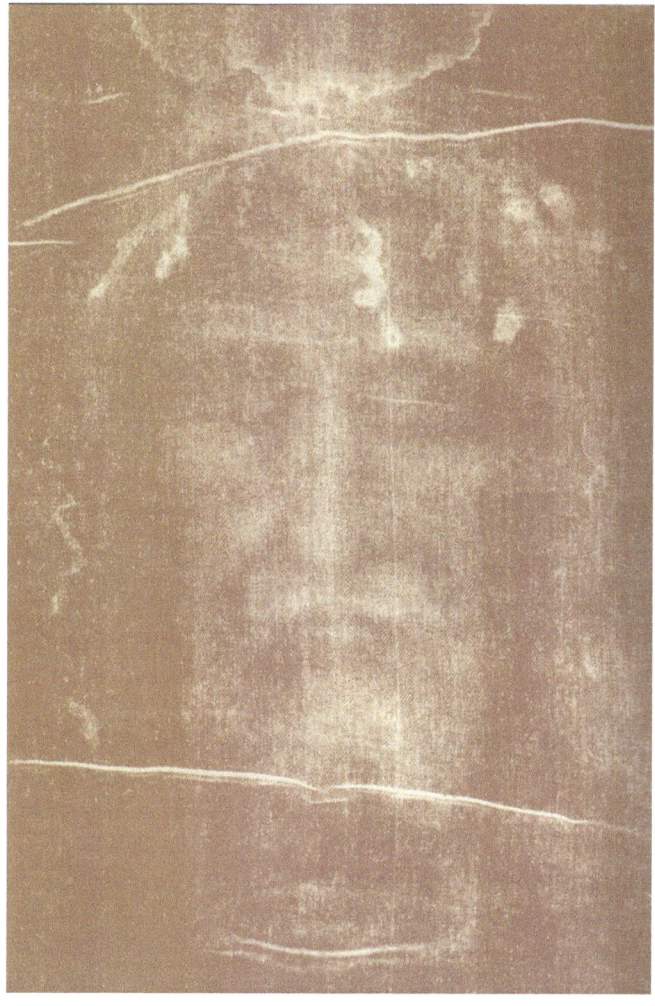

Figure 8: Secondo Pia's photograph of the Shroud[6]

by 60 centimeters (19.7 by 23.7 inches) in size, he was finally able to properly photograph the Shroud.

The first negative, which developed slowly as the plate was immersed in the processing bath – and which, in his excitement, he then almost dropped –

was to spread like wildfire throughout the entire world.

The photograph reveals long, perhaps wavy, hair; then the beard, flowing and thick, and the noble shape of the face; the eyes closed, the eyelids heavy.

The area above the right cheekbone appears to be swollen, as does the nose; the cheek is also swollen; it is the face of a person who has been injured. But there is no sign of muscular tension. The face appears unguarded and at the same time invulnerable, as if death had brought with it a miraculous peace. Secondo Pia's happiness at his extraordi-

Figur 9a: Original photograph of Shroud

nary photo was short-lived: no sooner had it been spread in the press throughout the world than two different fronts formed, each with a completely contradictory interpretation.

When the photographs brought to light the details of the markings on the Shroud, pathologists and forensic experts – including Barbet, Hynek and Sebastiano Rodante – examined the strange circle of wounds that appeared on the head. Paul Vignon had already clearly counted thirteen different-sized bloodstains on the forehead and temples, which were caused by thirteen different perforations of the skin. The blood had flowed from them unevenly: sometimes there were only a few drops (as if it were from broken capillaries), sometimes there was a larger stream of blood that had also clotted the hair; in other places it had run together and formed a long rivulet.

Where the back of the head, covered with thick long hair, had left its

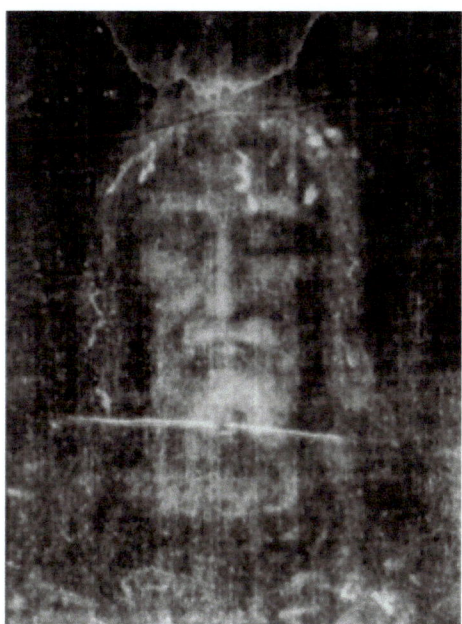

Figur 9b: Original photograph of Shroud negative

imprint, there were only large bloodstains and a small number of injuries, from which large, half-coagulated blood drops had formed on the Shroud. Altogether, a total of at least 30 wounds could be counted on the forehead, temples, and back of the head – arranged in an unusual and bizarre pattern. Rodante overlaid the imprints of the face on the Shroud onto anatomical plates that depicted the locations of the blood vessels. The blood clots on the forehead, where the greatest loss of blood occurred, corresponded to the frontal vein; the blood flow was therefore constant and viscous; other clots, coming from the frontal branch of the temporal artery, showed layers of successive phases of bleeding.

In the middle of the forehead a long, thick, and compact trail of blood could be seen, which made two sweeping curves before then returning to its vertical flow. It is a bizarre shape, difficult to interpret, which is why it became referred to as a "desperate fake."

Byzantine artists even interpreted it as a tuft of hair. But it wasn't hair – it was blood. Rodante identified it as being caused by a contraction of the forehead muscle, a convulsive reaction to the constant pain caused by the barbs in the crown of thorns.

And indeed, laboratory experiments have shown that when a viscous liquid is poured onto the forehead and the muscle is randomly contracted – as it is when someone tries to free their head from a tight grip

– deep wrinkles appear, out of which the liquid runs, spreads out, and leaves a pattern very similar to the one on the Shroud.

This last detail is almost excessively intense in its realism and can lead to a physical understanding of the torture that is much more haunting than abstract literary ideas.

The Death of the Man in the Shroud

According to the coroners' diagnosis, the man in the Shroud died of a pericardial tamponade, a rupture in the wall of the heart. In this type of death, as soon as the wall of the heart is torn and blood begins to pour into the pericardium, the dying person will utter a piercing scream. The Synoptics mention just such a scream (Mark 15:37; Matthew 27:50; Luke 23:46).

When a person dies from a rupture of the heart wall, if the heart is then punctured from the outside, blood and serum flow will from the wound. The blood that accumulates in the pericardium does not coagulate but breaks down into blood and serum. John testifies to this event as an eyewitness. The flow of fluids from the heart is evidence that the man in the Shroud had already died on the cross (John 19:34). If Jesus had still been alive, the soldier responsible for overseeing the orderly execution would have broken his legs, just as had been done with the two thieves crucified with him. No trace of anything like this can be found on the Shroud – just as is written in the Gospels: "[...] they did not break his legs." (John 19:33)

Jesus' sweating of blood in the Garden of Gethsemane on the Mount of Olives, as described in the Gospels (Luke 22:44), is one of the symptoms of extremely high blood pressure, which can trigger a heart attack. On the Mount of Olives, Jesus' soul struggled fiercely and battled within itself to carry out the will of the "Father" or "Love" within Him, despite the horrible suffering that he could so clearly see before Him. Many people question and doubt the necessity for Jesus to endure such an extremely cruel and painful death. However, this death was a completely voluntary sacrifice on the part of Christ. It is important to remember that God absolutely and completely respects the free will of humankind. The caste of priests who ruled at that time vehemently demanded the death of Jesus. In their opinion, if He were truly the Messiah, He would rise from the grave. So, they thought, why not test this out, and see if He was indeed the Messiah? They accused Jesus of insurrection against Caesar. By threatening Pontius Pilate that they would tell the Holy Roman Emperor that he was tolerating a rebellion against him, they forced Pilate to hand Jesus over to them to be crucified (John 19:13–16).

Jesus's crucifixion shows that out of God's great love for us, His desire for our salvation, His wish for us to become His free children, He was willing to make the most extreme of all conceivable sacrifices to His human body and soul. A person can only become a child of God through the independent exercise of free will, not influenced by external coercion. It is therefore not appropriate to blame God for the often alarmingly critical state of affairs that exists in the world today. It is the free will of all human beings that is responsible, and we must remain conscious of this in every such situation that has been brought about by human actions. God's greatest and most solemn commandment can be especially helpful in this regard: to God, loving our neighbor is evidence that we also love Him (see p. 217).

Determining the Date of Origin

During the course of scientific research on the Shroud, a controversial radiocarbon dating process was implemented in 1988, which established the Shroud as a forgery dating back to the Middle Ages. To correct the radiocarbon dating, in 2014, Giulio Fanti, Professor of Technical Chemistry at the University of Padua, together with Pierandrea Malfi, published a new book on the Shroud of Turin, entitled *La Sindone: primo secolo dopo Cristo!* (*The Shroud: The First Century After Christ!*)

A research project at the University of Padua had enabled the development of alternative dating methods for the Shroud of Turin, based on mechanical and optochemical analyses. These methods for dating ancient textiles are much more accurate than any previous procedures and would be able to eliminate any remaining doubts concerning the age of the Shroud. Fanti and his colleagues developed these methods, which allow the fabric to be examined without any risk of damage. This made it possible to obtain results within a much narrower time frame. The techniques employed were based on a combination of Raman spectroscopy and infrared spectroscopy with Fourier conversion (FTIR). The results obtained were all compatible with one another and, based on a variability range of 250 years, the mean value obtained was the year 33 A.D. This study was published in 2014 in the prestigious scientific journal *Vibration Spectroscopy*, and Professor Fanti also wrote about this in above-mentioned book. The February 25, 2014 issue of the magazine *Vatican Insider* featured an interview with Professor Fanti about his book.

The following is an excerpt from that interview, published with kind permission of *Katholisches Magazin fuer Kirche und Kultur*.[7, 8,]

Vatican Insider: Why the exclamation mark in the title?

Fanti: In itself it's an absurdity, because my dating could be wrong. However, I have intentionally set in response to what happened after the radiocarbon dating of 1988, when the scientists who participated in a published „final" result, which should no longer be debatable to some extent. But from a scientific point of view there is offered nothing that would not be debatable. And so it was, too. They were wrong. The scientists then could be photographed in front of a blackboard where they had written the result of their radiocarbon dating, which was provided with an exclamation mark. In response to this photo, I have now set as an exclamation mark in the title of our book: a small provocation.

V.I.: The radiocarbon dating from 1988 decreed that the grave cloth came from the Middle Ages. You say that's not true. But could not be wrong and your new dating?

Fanti: We know that the radiocarbon dating from 1988 is wrong. This was verified by a series of articles in international journals. The former dating left some aspects out of consideration, as well as the phenomenon of fire. According to the analysis of 1978 and 1988, the grave cloth was exposed to the monoterpene thymol, a very strong bactericide, however, the C-14 content changes, especially on old textiles. From a chemical point of view, therefore, you know: the grave cloth of a C-14 analysis should now again be subjected to the action of thymol would be reflected on the dating. I say this not to criticize what was done back then. However, the grave cloth may thus have rejuvenated in the course of twenty or thirty years. In light of what has happened in these recent decades: Who can tell us that the grave cloth was not stored in the first millennium with any preservative which has had significant impact? Today we know in any case that the radiocarbon date for the grave cloth poses systemic problems, because of the natural decay process is theoretically constant, but may have been changed by external events, of which we have no knowledge. Therefore, we have developed these alternative datings. I was able to systematize various methods scientifically and confirm this with what the American chemist Ray Rogers had established several years ago by an analysis: the grave cloth is older than the Middle Ages. I present in the book, three independent methods, but the results all agree with each other. All date the grave cloth much earlier than the radiocarbon analysis, and well before the Middle Ages, namely the first Century after Christ. Today, we have thus five different dating methods: the radiocarbon method, my three and those of Rogers. Also, we could have been wrong. But four different independent methods, reach the same result, but then speak a clear language. As long as these results are not refuted, and I can not imagine how this should be possible, these results have scientific validity. So that has first Century after Christ the greatest probability as emergence period for the Turin grave cloth. This dating corresponds exactly to the time Jesus of Nazareth lived in Palestine. We now await the reactions from the rest of the science world. So far we received only affirmative and affirmative responses, but no refutation.

V.I.: But who is the man depicted on the grave cloth?

Fanti: If we stay in a scientific context, we can not give him a name. However it is interesting that all the indications – and there are a total of hundreds - at a certain point it affirms a certain person and describes him. For example, to simply pick out a sign: The Romans crucified thousands of people, which is why the man of the grave cloth could be one of those many. But this is not so, because the crucifixion of the man on the shroud was special, and it is hard to imagine that other crucifixions have just taken place, as they have already described in the first century: it is the head wounds of a crown of thorns, the crucifixion was a punishment in itself, in the case of Jesus, however, there was the punishment of flagellation, because Pontius Pilate wanted to punish him really hard to release him, but instead it was a double punishment. The man of the linen cloth also has the wounds of a hard-flagellation. This double punishment was unusual for the Romans, as illogical as the higher punishment was the death penalty anyway. Like these there are many other clues. In order not to believe, a man must in view of the evidence and facts in abundance muster all his will already.

V.I.: How can the representation of man have arisen on the linen cloth?

Fanti: Since there is still no way to repeat the process, the formation can not be explained with scientific clarity. **At the current state of knowledge it seems to have been a burst of energy that came from the inside of the wrapped body. This energy was probably electrical and developed a special phenomenon, the coronal discharge is called (a myriad of micro-discharges between electrodes of a very high potential).** While there are scientifically significant difficulties to imagine the environment in which this phenomenon could take place (very strong earthquake or lightning), everything is explained exactly from the perspective of the Catholic religion. The Resurrection, with the consequent exit from the shroud, which was mechanically transparent. This is not the „fantasy" of any slight believing fideists, but supported by plentiful scientific evidence. On one hand we have the testimony of eyewitnesses and a contemporary written document. And we have the grave Shroud of Turin as well. The results are compatible and are also scientifically sound matches.

V.I.: What evidence do you mean in particular?

Fanti: For example, the human blood, liquefied again in the shroud, as this was exposed to the humid atmosphere of the tomb. A phenomenon that is called fibrinolysis and has left the marks on the linen fabric without the slightest trace of blurring, which would, however, have been self-evident and inevitable if the wrapped corpse physically moved and would have been unwrapped from the linen cloth. **There are two different layers of the grave cloth around the man's body recognizable: one that was more tightly wound during the emergence of the blood, a flatter, which goes back to the energy discharge through which the only "photograph" that Jesus left us about Himself and His painful Passion.**

Today, most scientists tend to hold that there was an inexplicable occurrence of radiation, since even in those parts of the body where the Shroud did not come into contact with the body, there is an image. In 2002, Fanti made an amazing discovery: he found that there are also very faint images of the face and hands on the back of the Shroud in the exact area where the face and hands are located. In other words, there is an image on the surface of both the front and back of the Shroud in these places, but the fibers between them have not been altered. This phenomenon indicates that there was radiation or an illumination of the body.

Supplemental Historical Information from the Sudarium of Oviedo

There is additional independent quantifiable verification of the authenticity of the Shroud of Turin. Research and analysis have revealed parallels between the Shroud of Turin and the Sudarium of Oviedo (*Santo Sudario*, meaning "shroud of sweat") in Oviedo, Spain. The Sudarium was first mentioned in the "Chronicum Regum Legionensium" of

Bishop Pelagius (d. 1153 A.D.) of Oviedo. According to that document, the Sudarium has been in Oviedo since the year 616 A.D.

According to experts, the Sudarium was used to cover the face of Jesus prior to his burial. The blood on the blood-soaked cloth belongs to the blood group AB, as does the blood on the Shroud of Turin. A pollen analysis of the Sudarium by Max Frei-Sulzer has confirmed the origin and the travel route of the Shroud. His analysis found pollen from Jerusalem, North Africa, and the Spanish cities of Toledo and Oviedo.

All of the markings correspond nearly perfectly to the face, beard, and hair of the man in the Shroud. The stains are composed of six parts pulmonary edema fluid and one part blood. This apportionment of body fluids occurs only when the deceased person has suffocated. The morphology of the stains indicates that the body was suspended in a vertical position from both arms. The head was inclined 70° forward and 20° to the right. It is clear that this was the victim of a crucifixion. If the corpse were to have been moved in any way, the fluids would have run out of the mouth and nose. These fluids, which were absorbed by the linen, make

Figure 10: The Sudarium of Oviedo[9]

up the majority of the stains visible on the cloth. Some of them are overlaid with clearly defined edges and there are a variety of shades.

On this basis, it was possible to calculate the time that would have elapsed between the formation of each stain. The previous stain would have had to have been completely or at least partially dry in order for the subsequent stain to be recognizable. In accordance with the Jewish tradition of covering the disfigured face of a dead person, the Sudarium was used to cover the bloody face of Jesus while His body still hung on the cross. The Sudarium's dimensions of approx. 84 by 53 cm (33 by 21 inches) testify to its Jewish origin. Its width corresponds to the old Jewish cubit measurement of approx. 50 cm (20 inches).

The stains on the Sudarium progressively reveal what took place with the corpse following death. The man had to have been already dead at the time the cloth was placed on his head, because, had he still been breathing, it would have been impossible for the stains to appear in the formation they did. While the man was still in an upright position, the primary stains initially occurred around the upper lip, cheek, chin, and beard. The back of the head exhibits a number of puncture wounds that were made while the man was still alive, and which were still bleeding until about an hour before the head was covered. These punctures are congruent with the wounds to the back of the head that are depicted on the *Sindone* (Shroud). They are most likely the wounds to the scalp caused by the crown of thorns, since the tip of a thorn was also found in the fabric of the Sudarium. After the body had been removed from the cross, the executed man was laid on his right side for some time, during which time a large amount of blood streamed from his nose and mouth, causing the distinctive stains on the cloth. The stains show that the left hand of another person tried to stop the flow of liquid: the marks left by this hand can be found in different positions around the bridge of the nose.

Perhaps this hand belonged to the Virgin Mary. For a further exploration of this, here is an excerpt, based on German-language mysticism, from Antonie Grossheim's booklet *Die sieben Worte Jesu am Kreuz* (*The Seven Words of Jesus on the Cross*), Chapter 4, p. 7:[10]

> IV. My Death and Removal of My Body from the Cross
> 1] After this My last word, I died, or rather: My soul stepped out of matter and unified himself with My Initial Spirit, who was the eternal Spirit of God.

2] And I descended to the place where the souls of the patriarchs were waiting for the hour of salvation, for no creature could enter the peace of Heaven before the justice of God was reconciled by the great work of love of salvation. So I freed the way again that was originally given to all beings but was once destroyed by the fall of the angels.

3] Adam had to repair that way again and had to lead the solidified matter, which enveloped all spiritual life, back to its beginning, for which reason the freedom of will was given to him. But he lost that freedom again by the sin of disobedience against God and fell again with all descendants ever deeper into judgment and death out of which there was forever no more hope for salvation. Then appeared the infinite Mercy and Love of the Eternal as Mediator and the Son of man, covered in the matter of the Earth, to free His creatures and lead them back to their fist and eternal destination.

4] When I hung on the cross, according to the prescribed Jewish law, the hour had come on which the bodies of the three criminals, among also I was counted, had to be taken off the cross, for it was the time of the day of rest when nobody was allowed to remain on the spot of execution. Then came My friends, who were mostly Romans and Greeks – also a few Jews were among them as My secret followers of My teaching – and they wanted to show their love for Me for the last time on Earth.

5] They bought My body from the supreme governor to be able to put it in the grave. And so, with mockery and scorn of the Jewish people, I was taken off the cross by the few friends who still remained faithful to Me. **And My mother, who was saddened unto death, fell before Me on the ground. And when she saw her child, mutilated, bleeding and dead, she took My head on her lap under intense lamenting and countless tears.**

Once Jesus' body had been brought to the tomb, the cloth was removed from His head and laid aside. For Orthodox Jews, nothing could have impurified them more than contact with blood or a bloody corpse. John specifically mentions that Jesus was buried in accordance with Jewish burial customs (John 19:40) and emphasizes that the Sudarium was folded up and placed in a special location. The use of the Sudarium has its origins in the aforementioned "Jewish burial customs." In the tomb, the Sudarium no longer covered the head of Jesus, as was long assumed on the basis of John's account of Lazarus' resurrection (John 11:44), but instead was placed to the side.

We may therefore reasonably conclude that the Shroud of Turin and the Sudarium of Oviedo are two complementary relics. The notion that there were two shrouds provides us with an explanation of the meaning of the passage in John 20:7. These two relics must be studied in combination. The significance for the dating of the Shroud is obvious.

Facts About the Shroud

The findings from well over one hundred thousand hours of scientific research are as follows:

➤ The Shroud dates from the first century A.D. Four different scientific methods were used to confirm this dating. The fabric consists of pure linen and was woven in a 3-to-1 twill weave. Samples of stone dust from the cloth contain the very rare travertine aragonite. This type of stone is indicative of the ancient burial sites around Jerusalem. The coins believed to have laid been on the eyes, a "simpulum" on the right and a "dilepton" on the left, would have been minted around the year 30 AD.

➤ The Shroud depicts the image of a crucified man and displays all of the traditional elements of the crucifixion of Jesus as described in the Gospels. The man had been flogged and then nailed to a cross for his execution, he wore a crown of thorns, and his heart was punctured by a stab wound after his death. From this wound, blood and serum flowed out of the body. The blood on the Shroud was found to belong to the blood group AB, but there were ambiguities with regard to the gender chromosomes (refer to the chapter on "The DNA Findings from the Shroud and the 'Virginity of Mary,'" p. 122). There is no contradiction between the findings from the Shroud and either Jewish burial practices or the texts of the Gospels.

➤ The pollen analysis of the linen fabric confirmed the established history of the Shroud and its journey. Microbiologist and criminologist Dr. Max Frei-Sulzer was able to identify pollen from 58 different plant species. Of these, 44 species are typical for the type of flora found around Jerusalem. The research undertaken by Professor Fanti then further confirmed these findings.

➤ In the Eastern Orthodox Church tradition, the story of the Shroud from the time of its transfer to Edessa is well known. The "face of Christ not made by human hands" is still mentioned in the texts for the consecration of icons, along with the name of King Abgarus. In ad-

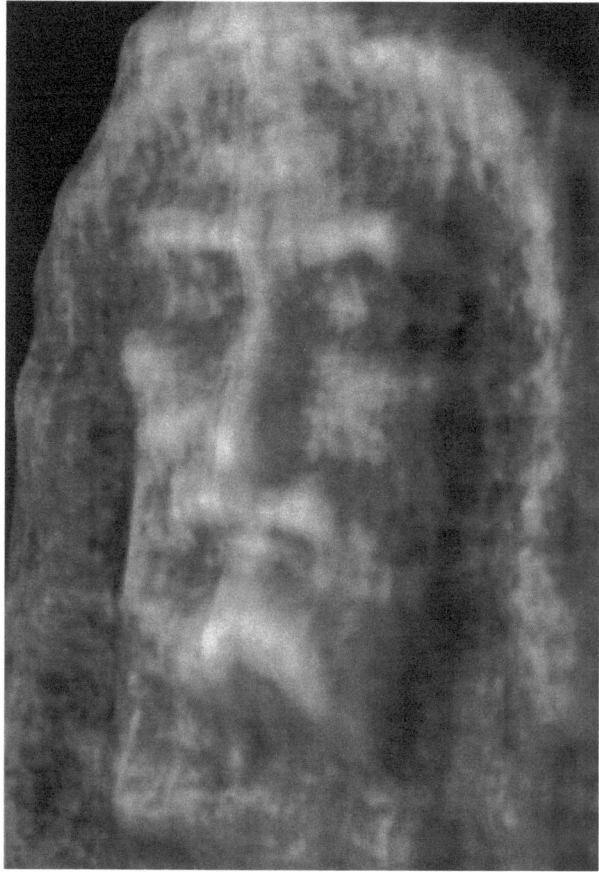

Figure 11: Three-dimensional rendering of the face
from the Shroud (M. Azevedo)[11]

dition, the British historian Ian Wilson has suggested that the Shroud
and the Mandylion of Edessa are identical. The Mandylion was
brought from Edessa to Constantinople in 944. The western world has
known of the existence of the Shroud since the conquest of Constantinople in 1204 and its later appearance in 1353 in Lirey, France.

➤ The image on the Shroud is not the work of an artist but was instead created by an energy form that has not yet been able to be identified by science. The imprint on the fabric is merely superficial and was not produced by pigments but by the discoloration of individual fibers.

➤ The overall image is the result of a combination of discolored fibers and bloodstains on the fabric. In the areas where the bloodstains are located, there are no traces of the image; the bloodstains occurred through fibrinolysis of the blood that had clotted on the body, and this took place prior to the creation of the image. The bloodstains correspond to the injuries reported to have been inflicted during the Passion, including the flogging, the crown of thorns, the crucifixion and the stab wound to the side following death, which pierced the pericardium. Analysis of the blood has also revealed an elevated concentration of bilirubin, which occurs when the blood in the veins decomposes while the person is still alive. This phenomenon generally occurs in situations in which a person experience severe, traumatic stress.

➤ The fact that the nails were driven through the wrists for the crucifixion is not reflected in conventional artistic representations of the Crucifixion, but it is consistent with experiments conducted in the 1930s by Pierre Barbet on corpses and amputated limbs.
Had the nails been driven through the palms of the hands, they would not have been capable of holding the body weight of the crucified person.

➤ Photographic image analyses have revealed the Shroud to be a photographic negative containing all the information necessary for creating a three-dimensional representation of the body that had been wrapped in it. Up until now, it has not been possible to clarify and decipher all of the facts. Even with all of our advanced modern knowledge of physics and chemistry, it is still not possible today to reproduce the image in a way that is true to the original.

---

1   Modern photograph of the Shroud, Guiseppe Enrie, public domain. https://en. wikipedia.org/wiki/File:Shroudofturin.jpg (accessed Sept. 7, 2020).

2   https://www.shroud.com/pdfs/guscin3.pdf (accessed Sept.7, 2020).

3   Translated from the Greek by Mark Guscin in *The Sermon of Gregory Referendarius*. https://www.shroud.com/pdfs/guscin3.pdf (accessed Sept. 7, 2018).

4   Hagion Mandylion, public domain, anonymous – Tretiakov Gallery, Moscow, https://commons.wikimedia.org/wiki/File:Christos_Acheiropoietos.jpg (accessed Sept. 11, 2020).

5   All excerpts were taken from Maria Grazia Siliato's book: *Und das Grabtuch ist doch echt. Die neuen Beweise*. Translation by C. Dyre.

6   Shroud of Turin (Secondo Pia), https://commons.wikimedia.org/wiki/Category: Shroud_of_Turin?uselang=de#/media/File:Shroudofturin1.jpg (accessed Sept. 11, 2020).

7   https://katholisches.info/2014/02/25/das-turiner-grabtuch-ist-echt-drei-neue-datierungsmethoden-weisen-ins-1-jahrhundert/ (accessed Dec. 15, 2020).

8   http://www.theeponymousflower.com/2014/02/the-shroud-of-turin-is-real-three-new.html (accessed Dec. 15, 2020).

9   Image of the Sudarium of Oviedo, Gino Moretto: *Das Grabtuch, Anleitung*, p. 56.

10 http://www.novorazodetje.si/7-words-on-the-cross/ (accessed Dec. 15, 2020).

11 Fanti, Giulio, *La Sidone*, p. 215.

The Shroud and Mysticism in the German-Speaking World

My Own Shroud Story – Discovering the Symbols on the Face of Christ

To help make our book and its spiritual assertions easier to understand, here is a brief overview of how it came to be: In the 1980s, as I was pursued my spiritual search for God and for truth, I came across Oswald Scheuermann's little booklet *Das Tuch* (*The Shroud*), in which he describes the Shroud of Turin. I was utterly fascinated by his writings and, convinced of the truth of its contents, I set out in search of additional signs of Jesus in our world.

In the 1980s, the Internet and the widespread access to information it allows was just beginning to become a part of our lives. It was not as easy then as it is today to find information on the Shroud. In those days, even just obtaining a decent photograph of the Shroud was no easy task in Protestant northern Germany. I wanted to hang a picture of the image of Christ from the Shroud on my wall, so I photocopied the very small image printed in Oswald Scheuermann's book (p. 33), re-copying and enlarging it several times until it was the right size.

In the process of making these multiple copies, the imprecision of the copying technology caused the image to become became more and more abstract, which allowed its symbolic content to become visible. Depending on which copying method was used, either the cross or the symbols in the blood would appear in the foreground.

Soon, and for many years, the image, in this simplified form, reduced to its most essential elements, hung before my eyes. It was an emotional relief to me that the foreground of the picture no longer fixated on the visible brutality of the torture that had been inflicted upon Jesus. The picture's "emblems" became a spiritual truth for me, and the symbols and their deep meanings have been forever etched in my mind. Since that time, throughout my life, this image of Christ has remained with me. I feel peace and protection when I stand before His image. In direct,

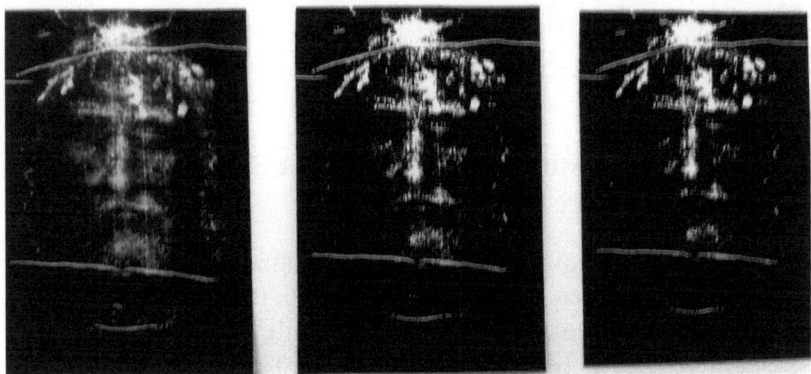

Figure 12: Author's enlarged photocopy of the Shroud negative

intimate, heartfelt conversation with Jesus, I find comfort, guidance and help for my life.

As I continued my search for Jesus in our world, I soon came upon the books of the "New Revelation," in which Jesus Himself, speaking through various prophets, describes His life and teachings very precisely. To find answers to my questions, I examined the connection between this relic and the writings of the mystics I had been reading, looking for any mutual affirmation. I continued to keep track of the ever-evolving scientific research on the Shroud and also visited the exhibitions in Turin. This book is the result of my many years of research.

Meditating on and contemplating the image allows many possible associations to be made with the spiritual content of the Shroud, for this image, the "Mandylion" of ancient Christian tradition, is still, by virtue of its authenticity, just as "miraculous" today as it was then. If people of faith devoutly worship the face from the Shroud, Christ Himself is able to bring about a new evangelization through his personal contact with the individual believer and to send out his Holy Spirit. There are even unique examples of this power held by the Shroud among atheist scholars who have researched it. Their intensive study of this holy object inspired them to believe in Jesus Christ.

Figur 13: Russian icon with Shroud

The ancient central Russian household icon in Figure 15 likewise portrays the strong power held by the authentic image of Christ. Entitled "The Archangel Michael and his Companions," we see the "Commander of the Heavenly Host and Standard-Bearer of Christ," surrounded by saints Blasius, Modest, Florus, and Laurus. The archangel, recognizable by his two golden wings, holds a painted copy of the "Mandylion," depicting "the image of Christ not made by human hands." Holding a corner of the cloth in each hand, he displays it to those around him. The halos of the "companions" surrounding him signify that they, as human beings, live in a state of intense contact with God to determine their actions and the manner in which they lead their lives.

According to the sacred "Legenda Aurea," in the Old Testament, the archangel Michael (Hebrew for "Who is like God?") is the protector and advocate of Israel. In the New Testament, he is the advocate for all of Christianity and, in particular, is the guardian angel of the German-speaking world. Michael is the angel of judgment and justice. He guards Paradise and symbolizes the Old Testament. He guides the souls of the dead to heaven, where he weighs them on his scales. Michael is an intercessor with God and a warrior against demons and the Antichrist.

Examples of Conscious Contact with Christ Through the Shroud

> *If you listen, you will sometimes hear a voice within you;*
> *it says, "I understand you," and other such things – accept this*
> *voice confidently for what it is: the voice of God.*
> Gerhart Hauptmann

Among the descriptions presented by Archbishop (emer.) Dr. Karl Braun and Dr. Barbara Stuehlmeyer in their book *Das Turiner Grabtuch, Faszination und Fakten* (*The Shroud of Turin, Fascination and Facts*) are the following:[1]

> Many theologians often reject it as an annoying nuisance – and sometimes as bitterly as if it were a threat to their employment.
> It is the sovereign, tranquil face in which everything that is true, good, and holy is gathered together. It is the hitherto undiscovered "philosopher's stone," which allows us to sense the metaphysical meaning behind the physical image.
> Seemingly out of nowhere, an inner dialogue with Christ takes place, with each observer perceiving His face differently.

> Looking at Him is not merely "informative," but "performative," in other words, it is life-transforming. And, it is not only individualistic; it calls us to accountability for the salvation of all.

In writing this very valuable book, these authors also followed a personal and spiritual call.

Professor Giulio Fanti

In a documentary by the German television broadcaster ZDF1, which has been re-broadcast several times, Professor Fanti describes yet another example of conscious contact with Jesus Christ through the Shroud of Turin.[2]

In 1968, as a 12-year-old child, Fanti visited the Turin Cathedral. The image of the Shroud made such an impression on him that he purchased a photograph of it for his room. In 1988, radio-carbon dating was performed on the Shroud. A headline claiming that the Shroud dated from the 14th century was immediately rejected by Fanti as being false. In 1998, now a physics professor, he visited the exhibition of the original Shroud, which is displayed only once every 25 years. In Professor Fanti's words:

"When I saw the Shroud for the first time, I felt a sense of the Eternal." Standing before the Shroud, Fanti wonders whether, in acting to prove the authenticity of the Shroud, he will be doing the right thing. "I asked the man on the Shroud an unambiguous question. As I stood there and gazed at the Shroud, I received a very clear answer. I felt it deep inside me. Clear and distinct!"

This religious experience was an affirmation to Fanti that he should move ahead with his plan to correct the results of radiocarbon dating.

General Thoughts

The profound disregard in which Christianity is held today puts a strain on the relationship with God that exists in our hearts. In the same way that we frequently lose the connection on our smartphones, the connection to our most important interlocutor is interrupted and damaged through denigration. Baseless disparagement cuts off the vital relationship to our Creator, significantly diminishing our pleasurable sense of inner tranquility and even making it inaccessible to many souls. Even the human conscience, that important voice from within our hearts, can become faint and almost inaudible through the defamation of the Christian faith. Also contributing to the problem is the partially mutilated and purposefully falsified handing down of the Word of God.

Voluntary unity under God's will could have a miraculous effect on our social fabric. Working together, with the power of the Holy Spirit, under His guidance within the boundaries of the laws of creation, we could bring about a positive transformation here on Earth. If we would allow ourselves to be guided by God's wisdom, we could achieve improved harmony among humankind and avoid much of the wasted effort and the splintering of communities that arises out of disputes. A peaceful uprising would bring about a commutated, meaningful movement towards the good.

My Personal Experience

I would like to recommend something to you, our reader, that will introduce you to a wonderful experience that is accessible to everyone. If you have not yet tried this, but feel an inner urge within you, then attempt to establish a direct spiritual connection to Jesus Christ by gazing at His image. My own experience over the years has shown me that almost every time I try to establish contact with Christ through His image or His word, I succeed in making an intense connection. Of course, I cannot make any great promises in this regard. I should probably also mention that repeated attempts at this could suddenly have a drug-like effect on you as well. Yes, apparently this, too, is similar to the modern smartphone. Some addiction researchers believe that smartphone use can lead us to become addicted to the neurotransmitter dopamine, with the feelings of happiness it triggers. I personally suspect that today's cell phone culture mimics the vital spiritual contact with God, replacing this contact with a plethora of information. This explanation helps me better understand much of the fascination with this technology.

As I have already written, if we human beings are to have a positive influence on our collective destiny, we need to re-establish a close relation-

Figure 14: When the bloodstains on the cloth are clearly depicted, the appearance of the image is horrifying. "The Shroud is a document of Jesus' love, written in blood"[3] (Pope Paul VI).

ship, free of fear, with the Holy Spirit, the Spirit of Love. Because God respects our free will, when we ask Him to, He helps us, so prayer is a particularly worthwhile activity for the children of God. Praying is also an opportunity for us to unburden our souls. It is vitally important that we come into the presence of God and His generous love. Here is what I believe: He knows how I feel and what I am worried about. He remains with me despite my weaknesses and He protects my life, my thoughts, and my prayer. Even in today's harried times, He guides me. He helps me to discern what is true and what is false and gives me peace and a clear conscience.

This personal, palpable, and supportive connection between our hearts and the spiritual realm helps us to more clearly understand the meaning of our life and struggles here on earth. This deeper understanding makes all of life's difficulties more bearable.

God truly is good to us and when we take the opportunity to speak with Him in our hearts, it leads to the joyful experiences that God wants to give us. Often, it is the lovingly grateful, silent, and devotional prayer that best helps us to attain divine comfort. I wish you much success and many moments of joy!

From the New Testament to the New Revelation

After two thousand years, only the Gospels have survived to this day. Frequently changing circumstances throughout history have meant that, with the exception of the New Testament, almost all of the records from the time of Jesus have been lost. In addition, some information has been distorted through human ineptitude.

In the first year A.D., the difficulties inherent in writing and reproducing long texts meant that the traditional Gospels could only be copied in a type of condensed version. The New Testament covers all of the essential points correctly. But only through "allegory" and "reading between the lines" can the true, deeper meaning be understood.[4] This historical necessity for creating abridged versions of the texts makes interpreting the Bible challenging.

Jesus later spoke through the prophets and their revelational writings to rectify possible misconceptions.

If people so desire, these can help them to find their way back to a true religion and a rational understanding of God. Detailed study of Jesus' teachings and His words, exactly as He gave them, will make it easier to gain a deeper understanding of Christianity. In John's Gospel (John 14:26), humanity is promised that as it continues to grow culturally and spiritually, additional explanations of the Christian doctrine and creation will be given from God:

> But the Comforter, which is the Holy Ghost, whom the Father will send in my name, he shall teach you all things, and bring all things to your remembrance, whatsoever I have said unto you.

Since the Holy Spirit was sent out only after Christ's ascension, this promise is for the future of Christianity beyond the death of Jesus. John 21:25 continues:

> And there are also many other things which Jesus did, which, if they should be written every one, I suppose that even the world itself could not contain the books that should be written.

And, John 16:12–15 tells us:

> [12]I have yet many things to say unto you, but ye cannot bear them now. [13]Howbeit when he, the Spirit of truth, is come, he will guide you into all truth: for he shall not speak of himself; but whatsoever he shall hear, that shall he speak: and he will shew you things to come. [14]He shall glorify me: for he shall receive of mine, and shall shew it unto you. [15]All things that the Father hath are mine: therefore said I, that he shall take of mine, and shall shew it unto you.

Here, Jesus is describing the work to be done by future prophets and apostles, who will reveal to us in His name what it is, beyond the Gospel, we need for the times in which we live and for our salvation. In German-speaking countries, part of this prophecy was fulfilled in the second half of the nineteenth century with the New Revelation. Through the inspiration of the Holy Spirit, Lorber, Mayerhofer and the other mystics proclaimed divine truths. Among these is a comprehensive account of the teachings of Jesus and the exact circumstances of both His life and that of His family. As part of the revelation concerning the creation of the universe and the earth, there is also a description of what awaits us in the next world and in eternal life after death.

From the New Revelation to the Shroud Messages

The "Old Testament" is the story of God's people being led by God Himself. With the help of many prophets, God proclaims over and over again in contemporary language His will for the well-being of His people. It is unlikely that this process will ever cease, since the individual stages of human development also allow for greater and lesser distance from God and His will. This is also the way Christianity understands prophecy. Paul emphasizes: "Quench not the Spirit. Despise not prophesyings." (1 Thessalonians 5:19–20).

Prophecy rejects all human claims to power and acknowledges only the authority of God as a standard for the actions of individuals and nations. On God's behalf, prophets often had to harshly rebuke degenerate rulers and nations and threaten them with punishment from God. This may be the reason for the extreme resistance with which the prophetic exhortations were met. The prophets themselves often struggled to carry out their tasks. The "New Revelation," which does not mince words in rebuking the ills that exist at all levels of our existence, has also met with extreme resistance.

The purpose of this book is to assist its readers with the challenge of evaluating these God-given writings. It illuminates the congruence between the New Revelation and the early Christian traditions as depicted in the mosaics of Ravenna and the symbols on the Shroud of Christ.

In their texts, the most prominent mystics of the New Revelation describe the Shroud and the crucifixion of Jesus: In 1846, Lorber, who referred to himself as "God's Scribe," revealed in *The Correspondence Between Jesus of Nazareth and Abgarus Ukkama, Ruler of Edessa* that an EMBLEM would be created during the Resurrection, which would, immediately following the Resurrection, be delivered to King Abgarus in Edessa.

Antonie Grossheim, a friend and supporter of Lorber's, received prophecies in 1863, which were recorded in a document that is brief, but rich in content: *The Seven Words of Jesus on the Cross* describes Jesus' crucifixion, the torture associated with it, and His last words as a human being on earth in more detail than do the four Gospels of the New Testament.

From 1891 to 1893, as a continuation of the uncompleted work of Lorber, Engel wrote the final (11th) volume of The Great Gospel of John. It can thus be said that the account of Jesus' life in the New Revelation is more comprehensive and detailed than what is written in the traditional Gospels. The eleventh volume of the GGJ includes a brief description of the Crucifixion, the Resurrection, and the circumstances surrounding it. Engel wrote his work 27 years after Lorber's death. In terms of content, this volume serves as a supplement to the ten volumes written previously. The only difference is the linguistic style. The eleven volumes of The Great Gospel of John should not be seen as a replacement for the New Testament Gospel of John, but as an illuminating complement.

Mayerhofer reveals to us the symbolic significance of the shape of the cross and the Crucifixion. Among his scientific writings, he describes how the shape of the cross can be found and where it appears in Creation and in the forms of all beings. We will come back to this later.

These texts were written before any scientific research had ever been conducted on the Shroud of Turin: it was not until 1898 that the first photographic negative and photograph were produced. Initially, even the photographic negative met with incredulity. No further research would be done until 1931. It goes without saying that the mystics could not have possessed any scientific knowledge about the Shroud.

Lorber's Abgarus Letter

In my opinion, the emblem represented by the Shroud had to have been planned over thousands of years – something that only God Himself would be capable of. During His lifetime, Jesus of Nazareth hinted to King Abgarus of Edessa that he could expect to receive an "emblem" of His resurrection. The source for this can be found in Lorber's *The Correspondence Between Jesus of Nazareth and Abgarus Ukkama, Ruler of Edessa.* The seven letters written by Jesus are a concise yet complete gospel, in which the proper handling of images of the Lord is also discussed. Skeptics may argue that this source is a pure product of the imagination, but let us review a few historical considerations.

In John 20:30, we read that the Savior did many things that were not reflected in the Gospels. For three years, Jesus preached, healed the sick, and performed miracles. How would it have been possible to document all this in the comparatively few pages that make up the Gospels? Of the many writings that were circulating at that time, only a few carefully selected ones were incorporated into the canon of the Bible. ("The canon" refers to the collection of those sacred texts that are considered inspired and are authoritative for our faith.)

The letters written by the King of Edessa to the "Miraculous Savior" Jesus of Nazareth were very likely not or no longer completely accessible to the Church Fathers at the time the Bible was compiled. Later, the prevailing theory was that the account of the Savior's correspondence was based on a local third-century legend that had originated in the Orient. This assertion may be based on the so-called "Decretum Gelasianum" (492–496 A.D.), which originated in the Frankish Church and contains a list of "books to be included." The Decretum placed the correspondence in the list of apocryphal books (writings of unconfirmed origin) that were not to be included.

Figure 15: "Thaddeus Presents Abgarus with the Image of Christ"[5]

Why was this correspondence not included in the Bible? It is a fact that historical evidence proves the existence of such an exchange of letters between Abgarus Ukkama and Jesus. It has been historically established that a king by the name of Abgar V Ukkama was the 15th sovereign ruler of the Kingdom of Osrhoene. According to the Chronicle of Edessa, he reigned over the fortunes of his country during two different periods: first, from 4 B.C. to 7 A.D., and then again from 13 A.D. to 50 A.D. In Lorber's *The Correspondence Between Jesus of Nazareth and Abgarus Ukkama, Ruler of Edessa*, Jesus says in his final reply:

> Do not fear the wooden cross to which I shall be nailed, because that very cross shall be, for all future times, the foundation and the door into God´s Kingdom. My body will be dead only for three days. On the third day I shall arise as the eternal overcomer of death and hell, and My almighty judgment will strike all perpetrators of evil. But for those who are of My Heart, I shall then open the gate of heaven wide before their eyes! When in a few days you will see the sun completely darkened by day, then be aware that I, your greatest friend and brother, died on the cross! - But do not be frightened by it! For all this must come to pass and still not a hair will be touched on the heads of those who are mine. **But when I will rise from the dead, at that moment you are to receive an emblem by which you will immediately recognize my Resurrection!** My love, mercy and blessing with you, my dear brother Abgarus! – Amen.

This clue reveals to us what was done with the Shroud following the Crucifixion. The facts are confirmed in the texts used by the Eastern Orthodox Church for the consecration of icons. Our knowledge of the events does not contradict the fact that the Shroud remained in Edessa for almost a millennium, from its creation until its transfer to Constantinople. It should be of great interest to scholars of the Shroud that this emblem from Jesus provides clear evidence of the Resurrection.

In Lorber's account of Jesus' correspondence with Abgarus, Jesus writes: **"But when I will rise from the dead, at that moment you are to receive an emblem by which you will immediately recognize my Resurrection!"** The Merriam-Webster dictionary defines "emblem" as "a device, symbol, or figure adopted and used as an identifying mark." The testament and **emblem** that God has given to us Christians and to all people through Jesus' death and resurrection, **is the Shroud, a testimony to the truth**.

The importance of preserving the Shroud until our day and age, when it would be possible for it to be scientifically examined, is also made evident in the following words of Jesus – found in Engel, GGJ 11, 76, 15 – as He speaks to his disciples about His appearance in physical form after the resurrection:

> In the midst of this gathering, which was also attended by Lazarus, I entered and greeted the assembled who, after their first surprise, thronged around me, overwhelmed by joy. This evening I once again taught them about the purpose of My death, as well as the teaching ministry now conferred upon them. I also admonished them to have no fear, since with a firm trust and with love for Me they were save from all persecutions. **Through my appearance I proved to them everlasting life in My Kingdom** and all were now completely filled with faith and eager hearts.

Mayerhofer also touches on this in *The Lord's Sermons*, No. 19, p. 116:

> The resurrection of the Lord:
> On earth, the keystone to the proof of My divinity was My raising from the dead; for without this My teaching, My deeds and My whole life would soon have been forgotten. My disciples would have broken up; they would perhaps still have been attached to Me for themselves, but they would no longer have been fruitful for their fellow men.

In 1988, the Shroud was declared a forgery. At the time, radiocarbon dating was in its infancy. The results it provided placed the Shroud's origins in the fourteenth century. Since then, however, scientists have spent hundreds of thousands of hours researching the Shroud with the aid of state-of-the-art technology and have confirmed its authenticity. Professor Fanti and his colleagues have, as already discussed, described the problems they encountered, and their findings have been confirmed by extensive research. Despite this, regrettably, the media repeatedly calls attention to "evidence that the Shroud is a forgery."[6]

What is completely unfathomable in discussions surrounding the Shroud of Christ and the research into its authenticity is the complete disregard for the invaluable traditions of the Eastern Orthodox Church. For example, in the texts used for the consecration of icons, with which I became familiar through my icon-painting courses, explicit reference is made to the "not-made-by-human-hands image" delivered to Abgarus:

> You taught us to worship the not-made-by-human-hands-image of our Lord Jesus Christ, which had been wonderfully imprinted by Him on a cloth and

sent to King Abgar of Edessa, and through which the King and many other sick people had been healed.

This text from the Eastern Orthodox Church also points to Lorber, who prophetically newly revealed these events in his *The Correspondence Between Jesus of Nazareth and Abgarus Ukkama, Ruler of Edessa.*

I believe that this "emblem" was planned in great detail over a very long period of time, because the origin of the commandment to Moses concerning the purity of fabrics for garments most likely dates back to the imprisonment of the Jews in Egypt. Perhaps it was necessary that pure flax fibers be used so that the image would be able to appear on the Shroud, something for which we still do not have a technical explanation.

The unusual and quite luxurious design of the Shroud created a fabric that is very smooth, dense, and durable. Obviously, for the fabric to survive for 2000 years, these special qualities were essential. "Blood shrouds" stem from the Jewish law requiring that persons who die violent deaths be buried together with their blood. The blood of the deceased was considered "living blood." It was not until today, 1,900 years after the Shroud's creation, that modern technology and science made it possible for additional data and information to be revealed. Future research will undoubtedly uncover still more secrets of the Shroud.

The Shroud of Christ and the New Revelation: Mutual Affirmation

In the following, I will present the details of the Crucifixion as they are recorded in the texts of the New Revelation. These details were largely unknown prior to the scientific analysis of the Shroud. As previously mentioned, the Gospels represent a type of "abridged version" of the story, conveying only the main points.

My own conviction – and the working hypothesis put forward at the beginning of this book – was: The New Revelation affirms the Shroud and, conversely, the Shroud affirms the New Revelation. On the assumption that both are God-given, we should be able to confirm their congruence.

For example, Jesus provided hints about how the image on the Shroud was created during His Resurrection. He describes the dematerialization of his body on the third day after his death. His description of the Resurrection, together with scientific insights from the New Revelation, could provide scientists with new clues to help to clarify the genesis of the image.

Here now is an overview of the parallels identified so far between the Shroud of Christ (SC), the corresponding scientific research results, and the accounts from the New Revelation (NR)[7], arranged chronologically according to the events of the Crucifixion and Resurrection. The Revelation texts provide many more details of the surrounding circumstances than do the traditional Gospels.

SC: The shoulders display orthopedic changes that could be expected to occur over the years in a carpenter who carried heavy loads. The right shoulder is lower than the left.

> **NR:** Lorber's *The Childhood of Jesus* provides detailed descriptions of the carpentry work done by Jesus and the heavy loads that had to be carried by members of Joseph's family from the time of Jesus' childhood until the beginning of His teaching ministry as the Messiah.

+

SC: The tortured man was almost killed by a severe flogging. The victim's body bears wounds from innumerable lashes of a whip. Scientists were able to identify at least 370 different lash wounds. Since not every part of the body is visible on the shroud, the number of lashes probably totaled about 600. Extremely severe blows, especially to the kidneys, can be fatal by sending a person into shock or causing spontaneous kidney failure.

NR (Grossheim, 2, 7):

> After I had suffered for a long period of time and with much pain which I had to endure by the tormentors who did not spare their efforts, the high priests saw that **I might die** before they could have cooled down their vengeance and rage on Me, and they tried to receive the death sentence as soon as possible from the highest Roman Court in order to still be able to taste of the joy to see Me die as painfully as possible. When the message of My death sentence arrived, which said that I had to be crucified, My enemies rejoiced loudly and they tried to carry out their work as soon as possible.

+

SC: The hands showed signs of having been shackled.

NR (Grossheim 3, 1):

> When the cruel tormentors robbed My clothes and, naked, they **tied My hands** and feet **to the wood** and also pierced them with many blunt nails, it happened that My tortured body sighed and said: "Father, forgive them, for they do not know what they are doing."

+

SC: The Shroud shows forensic evidence of an incredibly brutal torture, including many injuries over the entire body.

NR (Grossheim 3, 2):

> When I was thus raised on the cross, My body, covered with blood and dust, looked so pitiful that it touched even the heart of the enemies who were present.

+

SC: Pathologists have determined that death was most likely caused by a heart rupture, i.e. the rupture of the heart muscle. This is suggested by the condition of the dried bodily fluids from the pericardium at the wound in the side. After death, the solid and liquid components of the blood in the body would have separated and, as a result of the subsequent stab wound, would have settled clearly and distinguishably on the body and then on the Shroud.

NR (Lorber, *Gifts of Heaven*, Vol. 1 "The Suffering of the Lord"):

> But because the humanly suffering ego included in itself another divine ego, this suffering was also a twofold one, namely the outer bodily and the inner divine ego. This suffering lasted until the point when I exclaimed on the cross: "It is finished! Father, into your hands I commend My Spirit!" – or in other words: "Behold Father! Your love comes back to You!"– and as soon as the infinite power of God **tore apart all ties of death and Hell.** Eternal power stormed out with infinite violence. The whole earth shook, moved by the omnipotence of God. Voluntarily, it opened its graves and drove the prisoners to life.

+

SC: The **wound to His side** was inflicted upon Jesus after He had died. **The separation of the blood and serum, which occurred after death,** is clearly identifiable by the nature of the stains on the Turin Shroud.

NR (Grossheim 4, 6):

[…] for this injury was only inflicted upon Me when I already had left My earthly body, and it was only the arbitrary act of a merciful soldier who thought that I was perhaps still in a powerless deadly struggle. Through that, he wanted to deliver Me earlier from My terrible suffering.

+

The Sudarium of Oviedo: Someone held Jesus' head while it was still wrapped in the Sudarium, but there are no signs of any great wiping or rubbing. On the fabric, it is clearly discernible that someone's left hand was trying to stop the seepage of the fluids.

NR (Grossheim 4, 5):

And My mother, who was saddened unto death, fell before Me on the ground. And when she saw her child, mutilated, bleeding and dead, she took My head on her lap under intense lamenting and countless tears.

+

SC: Traces of anointing oils have been found on the Shroud. Imaging of 31 different species of flowers and plants indicates that the Shroud had been strewn with a profusion of flowers. These gifts of love[8] obviously dematerialized along with the body, otherwise it would not be possible to detect the imprints, left by some type of electrical discharge. Perhaps due to a lack of time, as it was already late in the day, the body was only wrapped loosely in the Shroud and not bound tightly in it.

NR (Grossheim 5, 1):

Then I, meaning My physical body, was carried away to the grave that was located at quite a distance from the city of Jerusalem and belonged to the high priest Nicodemus. When My body, according to the custom of the Occident **well provided with spices and wrapped in white linen,** was sunk into the tomb, my friends surrounded Me weeping and lamenting.

+

SC: About 20 hours after death had occurred, the process of fibrinolysis caused the blood that had coagulated and become encrusted to become liquefied again, allowing it to be absorbed into the linen Shroud. To obtain the most precise blood imprint from fibrinolysis, the optimal time span is between 36 to 40 hours after death.

Based on this, we can draw some conclusions about the exact time of Resurrection. It follows that the Resurrection must have taken place between three and seven o'clock in the morning (see Professor Fanti's report).

NR (Grossheim, 5, 3):

Having lain in the grave about two days, the time of my Transfiguration (or Resurrection) had come, to fulfill the Scriptures. And when the morning dawned on the third day, it happened that, free from the ties of death and **uniting My soul with the transfigured body,** I arose to my heavenly Father (or the Original Spirit) and gloriously ascended as the Conqueror of death and Satan.

NR (Lorber, *The Correspondence Between Abgarus Ukkama…*, 7, 15):

My body will be dead only for three days. **On the third day I shall arise again from the death** in Jerusalem as the eternal Overcomer of death and hell, and My almighty judgment shall fall upon the evildoers!

+

SC: During the actual resurrection, the blood stains were not smeared in any way, as if the body were removed motionlessly from the Shroud. The body seemingly was levitating, because the profile of the back of the body is in no way flattened as would be the case when a body lies on a piece of fabric. The face is also faintly visible on the upper side of the Shroud. Some type of irradiation is assumed to be responsible for the formation of the image, although no scientific explanation has yet been found.

By 2012, on the basis of previous studies, Fanti had already identified 24 special characteristics of the Shroud. Two thirds of these meet the criteria for having been formed through radiation. These chemical and mechanical-based results are significant for the images on the Shroud of Turin, according to an article by Fanti in the *Journal of Imaging Science and Technology*, as reported by the magazine *Vatican Insider*.

Some of the interesting data include findings of a color depth of 0.2 micrometers in the outer layer of one of the Shroud's fibers and the phenomenon of the image appearing on the front and back of the cloth. However, Professor Fanti rejects radiation hypotheses that suggest that the energy required for this would have emanated from the body itself, such as in the so-called "corona effect." He considers a strong electromagnetic wave impulse in the UV range, which can be generated by a lightning bolt, during an earthquake, or by radon gas, to be much more likely.

The main issue is the amount of energy required. To create an image the size of the Shroud of Turin, **34 trillion watts** would be needed – **twice the energy output of the entire earth** in 2012. Only small, less than one-inch sections of the image could be reproduced at that time. The reproduction of the entire Shroud would require resources that were not available in laboratories. For the collaborative experiments conducted by Professor Fanti and Professor Giancarlo Pesavento, electrical currents of about 500,000 volts were needed to produce images only a few centimeters large that were similar to those on the Shroud. Obtaining an image the size of the entire Shroud of Turin would require several hundred thousand volts of electricity and, potentially, substantial quantities of radon gas. However, according to Fanti, if the legendary relic is indeed "a by-product of the Resurrection," no laboratory experiment will ever be successful.

NR (Engel, GGJ 11, 76, 1):

> **On the third day of Passover, the Deity returned** and called the body of the Son of Man, which **immediately dissolved completely** and was now added as the garment to the soul. The Roman guards saw this process as a **shining light** which frightened them so much that they ran away in haste to announce that I had risen from the dead. The stone was rolled away from the opening, so that now everyone could have a look into the tomb.

NR (Lorber, *The Correspondence Between Abgarus Ukkama...*, 37):

> But when I will rise from the dead, in that moment you shall receive an emblem by which you will immediately recognize My resurrection!

+

SC: The body was dead, there can be no question of any possible physical or human survival. This is proven by the condition of the dried body fluids, supported by the findings on the Sudarium of Oviedo.

NR (Engel, GGJ 11, 76, 2):

> The soldiers hastened to Pilate, who greatly amazed, informed **the Great Council** with a certain malicious pleasure. Soon some of its members went out and found the place empty, whereupon, **fearful of the people,** whose displeasure they knew, they anxiously tried **to cover up the matter,** because of the people whose anger they knew, gave money to the guards and demanded that they should say that **the disciples had stolen the body** while they slept.

+

On the topic of further "not-made-by-human-hands" images, the following statement appears in the New Revelation:

NR (Engel, GGJ 11, 74, 12):

> Jesus: "According to traditions of the church, the maid Veronica handed Me a cloth with which to wipe the sweat. This is quite true, for she stood in the front row of those lamenting. However, the imprint of My face in this cloth is a later legend."

The "Veronica legend," which tells of Jesus' face being pressed into a sudarium during the Passion, has only existed since the 12th century and only in the Catholic faith. The quotation above casts new light on speculations about the Veronica shroud. Jesus tells us unequivocally that the imprint caused by the sweat did not create another supernatural image of His suffering. Worshipping a false image of Jesus is unlikely to lead to direct contact with Christ. A falsified historical reproduction may lead believers astray and dissuade them from the Orthodox traditions that have preserved the roots of Christian tradition until today.

+

The revelatory details in the texts of the various mystics affirm this extraordinary "emblem" of Christianity, the Shroud of Christ, to be authentic and unquestionably genuine. Therefore, believers, deeply trusting in their own personal God, can also accept the spiritual content of the texts as having been affirmed to be credible.

Connections Between the Shroud, the New Revelation, and the Gospels

In my opinion, the "discernment of spirits" has become a very big problem in our day and age. The excessive proliferation of corrupt influences makes it difficult for divine inspiration to reach our hearts and minds without being distorted. This causes some believers to become afraid that they will be taken in by false prophets and evil spirits. It can make people who are seeking God feel unsure, because they can no longer be certain what the source may be for the flood of inspiration they feel in their hearts. Because He foresaw that all these many problems would arise in our time, Jesus left us His Shroud and ensured as early as the nineteenth century that the New Revelation would be given. In the sincere and loving worship of Jesus, the image of the Shroud can help people who are seeking to establish a personal relationship with God.

The best way to open your mind so that you can discern between good and evil as well as right and wrong is through prayer, requesting God's guidance.

Matthew 7:7–8:

> [7]Ask and it will be given to you; seek and you will find; knock and the door will be opened to you. [8]For everyone who asks receives; the one who seeks finds; and to the one who knocks, the door will be opened.

I am convinced that with the signs and symbols on his Shroud, Jesus is validating the texts of the New Revelation and affirming that these messages come from the realm of light.

From my perspective, the same applies to icons of Christ that have been copied from the original. In the Eastern Orthodox texts for the consecration of icons, the power of the Shroud is described through the description of the miracles in Edessa. In order to access this power, the icons of Christ based on the Shroud must be "copied verbatim." In Orthodoxy, the icons are understood to be "windows to heaven," simultaneously signifying the presence of the Being depicted, that is, the presence of Christ, as well as that of His Holy Spirit. When individuals worship Christ through his image, personally, faithfully, and in loving devotion, then, just as in the parable of the mustard seed, the true revelation of Christ through his Shroud can bear great spiritual fruit for every believer. As we read in Mark 4:30–34:

> The Parable of the Mustard Seed
> 30Again he said, "What shall we say the kingdom of God is like, or what parable shall we use to describe it? 31It is like a mustard seed, which is the smallest of all seeds on earth. 32Yet when planted, it grows and becomes the largest of all garden plants, with such big branches that the birds can perch in its shade."

> The Parables in Jesus' Teaching
> [33]With many similar parables Jesus spoke the word to them, as much as they could understand. [34]He did not say anything to them without using a parable. But when he was alone with his own disciples, he explained everything.

Clearly, the revelations of the mystics also contain certain weaknesses and errors. In the process of prophesying, these weaknesses can be transformed into revelatory utterances. As is written in 2 Corinthians 3:6:

He who has made us sufficient to be ministers of a new covenant, not of the letter but of the Spirit. For the letter kills, but the Spirit gives life.

Like a multi-colored lampshade, the Divine Light is individually tinted by the personality of the prophet before being transmitted to humanity. Jesus addresses this in the New Revelation, saying that it is his intention that there also be errors within the revelations, because otherwise, spiritually under the pressure of absolute truth, people would fall asleep. For the development of individual free will, each person must contribute by working to the best of his or her spiritual ability. At times, God has presented His communications about nature in such a way that some scientists have not been able to accept them until they relinquished their earthly intellect for spiritual wisdom.

Jesus said:

1. Behold, small is the heart of man, but the horizon of his feelings is much wider, if that being is in the power of faith from pure love towards Me. I assure you, there is no thing so hidden that cannot be touched by the rays of pure feeling; and when the pure rays of feeling have grasped something, ask yourself if it would still be possible to grasp the thing differently than it really is and exists in itself.

2. Quite different, of course, is the case with rational people. They hunt for all things with their short arm [of understanding], just as underage children hunt for the moon and other very distant things. These people then draw their feelings into their narrow minds and let them grope around in them like a blind man who has sat down on a block of stone carved with hieroglyphics and is grabbing at it without even a faint hint that these are hieroglyphics, and even less that this writing is a mysterious analogical language from the bright rays of pure feeling.[9]

Guidelines for testing prophetic statements.

[19]Do not quench the Spirit. [20]Do not despise prophecies, but test everything; [21]hold fast what is good. [22]Abstain from every form of evil. (Paul in 1 Thessalonians 5:19–22)

These words of Paul challenge us as Christians to cultivate a faith that is congruent with intelligence and reason. There is no mention of "blind faith" in the Holy Scriptures. God wants us to independently work out and expand our personal faith. Religious experts and secular leaders alike will, of course, object to the possibility that God speaks

Figure 16: Positive and negative images of the Pantocrator icon and the face of the man from the Shroud. We can see how the image of the icon becomes less meaningful in the negative image, whereas the negative image of the Shroud is easier for the human eye to interpret. The images are presented here mirrored, so as to facilitate comparison with the corresponding positive image.[10]

directly to His children. They will oppose it with every means at their disposal.

People must assert their God-given rights themselves. Jesus emphasized the equality of all people before HIM: "[...] you are all brothers" (Matthew 23:8). His words to each one of us were: "I will not leave you as helpless orphans" (John 14:18). So let us, each and every one of us, listen and hear God's message within us.

On the other hand, this truth must be emphasized: We can only truly and completely give what we ourselves possess. This applies at the spiritual level just as it does at the material one. This means that teachers who have no personal understanding of the truth and no deep insight into the spiritual realm will not be capable of teaching spiritual truths or helping others to access the spiritual realm. Since, as Jesus tells us, the Kingdom of God is spiritual in nature, anyone who focuses only on the material world and their own personal well-being will not be able to give an authentic account of the spiritual realm. This would be similar to the goats mentioned in Ezekiel 34:18–19, who foul the water:

> [18]Is it not enough for you to feed on the good pasture, that you must tread down with your feet the rest of your pasture; and to drink of clear water, that you must muddy the rest of the water with your feet? [19]And must my sheep eat what you have trodden with your feet, and drink what you have muddied with your feet?

Jerusalem's upper classes were unwilling to follow a – by the world's standards – impoverished and powerless Messiah. Because it was a spiritual kingdom that Jesus had established and because He was not striving for earthly dominion, he disrupted the elite classes' claim to power. This upper class expected the Messiah, as its leader, to rule with them over the entire known world as well as to liberate them from the Romans who dominated them. To maintain their own power, the ruling class had the Messiah executed. This made it impossible for many devout Jews to gain access to the proclaimed Messiah or to Heaven.

Our aim in calling to attention the mutual congruencies that have been described in the prophecies presented above is to make these texts accessible to the readers of our book as the true Word of God. This way, the Word of God can be used as a guide and a source of consolation and strength for our daily lives. Those who are seekers can love and worship the Shroud of Turin as the true image of Jesus, in gratitude for our redemption.

---

1 Translations of the excerpts by C. Dyre

2 Documentary from the German broadcaster ZDF: *Mythen-Jager: Das Turiner Grabtuch (Myth Hunters: The Shroud of Turin)*. Produktion: IMG Entertainment; World Media Rights GB 2014 in cooperation with ZDF Enterprises.

3 Quotation from "Der Turiner Dom und das Leichentuch von Turin" (*The Turin Cathedral and the Shroud of Turin*) from 1985. Image is property of the Turin Cathedral, Piazza San Giovanni – Torino / No further information available.

4 For a better understanding of how the terminology from the theory of allegory is used, examples can be found in the description of the Apse of Classe (see pp. 140–144, Figs. 27, 28, 29).

5 https://de.wikipedia.org/wiki/Abgarlegende, public domain

6 One example of this is the YouTube video: "New! The Secret 1982 Carbon Dating of Shroud" (https://www.youtube.com/playlist?list=PL2mAxwAyi4UpUMTReg1LTfU KgUEKpg__U)

7 The most important statements are highlighted in bold to provide a better overview. The text excerpts are very concise and contain only the main points. Reading the original texts will help the reader place the events in a wider context.

8 I find it very touching that God also dematerialized these flowers, this helpless expression of love from His friends, and "took them with Him" into His Kingdom.

9 Lorber: *Gifts from Heaven* Volume 3, *A Brief Epithet*. The dimensions of the human heart, feeling and mind. October 16, 1840, p. 65, 1-66, 6. See also the chapter on *Feeling and Understanding*, p. 252.

10 Fanti, Giulio, *La Sindone*, p. 61.

The Markings on the Shroud as Allegories

The Symbolism

The markings on the Shroud, created by Jesus' blood, can be considered to be allegories, that is, spiritual statements expressed by these "symbols of the Word." Blood symbolically represents the Spirit. What follows is an attempt to interpret the messages contained in markings on the Shroud, created in the blood of Jesus. Revelations 5:9–10:

> ⁹And they sang a new song, saying, "Worthy are you to take the scroll and to open its seals, for you were slain, and by your blood you ransomed people for God from every tribe and language and people and nation, ¹⁰and you have made them a kingdom and priests to our God, and they shall reign on the earth."

The traces of blood we will be examining appear as brighter areas on the photographic negative created by the image on the Shroud. Paul Vignon, one of the Shroud researchers, has identified thirteen different perforations to the skin of the temples and face, all of which left clear traces of blood.

The Number "3"

When looking at the image on the Shroud, we can see on the forehead a figure of the number "three," with a drop of blood suspended from it. This "three" is referred to as such in numerous publications about the Shroud and is often featured on their covers. In some of these images, the figure of the "three" is graphically enhanced, and sometimes even quite distinctly highlighted.

How was the "three" created? The extremely painful punctures in Jesus' scalp from the crown of thorns caused His forehead muscles to tense up. This torture forced Jesus to furrow his forehead. The blood flowed out over the creases in his forehead, forming the "three." Blood oozed out of an additional wound, congealed into a droplet, and became part of this symbol. On the face, the forehead is symbolic of the outwardly revealed spirit.

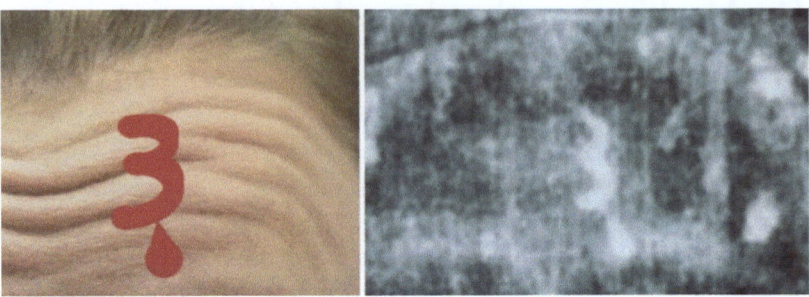

Figure 17: Furrowed forehead muscle with blood flow (Peter Kutzki)

This region of the face is also considered to be the seat of the mind. In nearly every culture, a furrowed brow is interpreted as rejection or concern. Similar to a seal, the "three" can therefore be understood as a confirmation. A seal has three attributes: name, title, and dominion, as seen, for example, in the titulary: Jesus of Nazareth, King of the Jews.

The "three" – if regarded, with the attached droplet, as a seal – could be interpreted as: **"Jesus Christ, the Godhead, incarnated as man and now the risen Lord of the universe,"** or, in Old Testament language: "Jesus Christ, Messiah of the Jews."

The numbers three and one are also reflected in the fabric from which the Shroud was made. The linen is a 3-to-1 twill weave in a herringbone pattern that was very rare and exceptionally precious in Jesus' day.

The Question of the "Trinity"

Jesus manifested himself on earth, embodying God's being. In this way, the infinite Spirit, who encompasses all dimensions, became visible to us in human form. Through His life as a human being, Jesus gave us the gift of a God who is visible and palpable. Until the Incarnation, no one, not even a spirit, had been able to see God. His finite creations were only able to perceive Him as a sea of light, not as an entity.

For Jesus's disciples, their three-year apprenticeship was fundamentally too short. Had Jesus revealed His omnipotence at the beginning of their time together, it would have been too overwhelming for His apostles. Therefore, and also because the spiritual freedom of His followers was important to Jesus, He at first only referred to Himself as the Son of God. We should perhaps acknowledge that even today, most people have not yet fully grasped the meaning and significance of their freedom of will. This will help us to understand why the Son, Holy Spirit, and God the Father have been erroneously thought of as separate entities.

The great significance of the question surrounding the "Trinity" is evidenced by the fact that it was specifically a symbol of the number "three" that Jesus consciously created on His forehead, and not any other other number. In allegorical fashion, the trail of blood on Jesus' forehead formed in a chronological sequence, just as the creation and fulfillment of God's self-representation as something we could understand required a time span of about 33 years. Creating the "eternal Christ" required the duration of his earthly existence for the spiritualization of his body. The single drop of blood located at the end of this trail of blood symbolizes that **the Risen Christ is the God we are able to understand and perceive.**

We can well understand God's frown if we examine the dramatic disputes surrounding the terms "trinity" and "triune" that have taken place over the many centuries of Christian history. This concept of a tri-theistic God, which even the Churches admit **is inexplicable and incomprehensible, yet which is still deemed "indispensable,"** has inflicted much suffering throughout the world. Within the theological edifice of the Western churches, this impious and incomprehensible concept stands in the way of di-

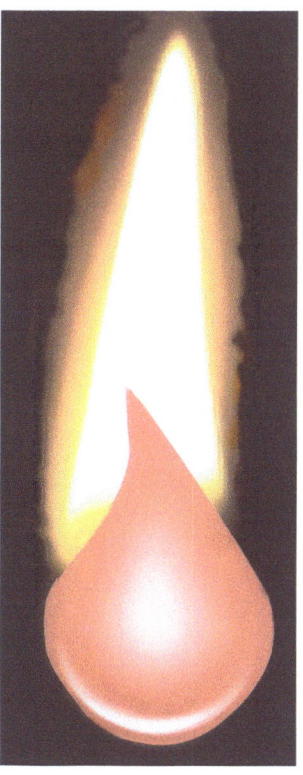

Figure 18: Flame and droplet of blood (Peter Kutzki)

rect personal contact between an individual and God. It prevents people from being able to experience God in a direct way, because it keeps them at a distance from Jesus. This theological division of the nature of God into three entities makes it difficult for believers to establish contact with the universal God. As a result, it is difficult for the power that flows from direct contact with God as Holy Spirit to flourish and work within them. This confusing and essentially meaningless concept robs our Christian "religion" of its inner power.

At several points in the New Revelation, Jesus, as recorded by Lorber, warns his disciples against the portrayal of God in three persons.

> Having been given the reason why, you will now also understand that the stating of the three names will hardly lead people to imagining three divine personages, provided you teach them truthfully and correctly. But I earnestly urge you to give the people everywhere a right and truthful light on this matter. Where it will be lacking, there men will easily and soon wither and go over into all kinds of false doctrines, and it will then be very difficult to lead them onto the path of full truth.
>
> Yet you will not be able to prevent that, notwithstanding your faithfulness, there will arise false teachers and prophets that you will certainly not be able to prevent. For this you will not be made responsible as also a farmer who sowed pure wheat on his field and for whom his enemy

Figure 19: An attempt ca. 1800 to represent the Trinity[1]

strewed weeds under it at nighttime, cannot be blamed if weeds grow in his field under the wheat and weaken the good fruit.

It is my love's desire that all men on earth enter upon the lightful paths of truth and walk thereon towards eternal life; but since, for reasons I have already announced to you, I have to withdraw completely with My omnipotence, every human being is completely free and may believe and do what he wishes.

In the spreading of my teaching you will have the most success when you work upon the peoples the intellect and mind.

Once the intellect and the mind have been permeated with the teaching, faith becomes alive and successfully active through good will.

If the mind and spirit are not properly enlightened, faith remains only a mute and blind acceptance of what man has heard from some authorized source.

Such a faith is hardly close to none; it does not stimulate the mind to a voluntary and joyous deed which makes the heart happy, and is therefore dead, because it is without spontaneous and joyful works. (Jesus to his disciples, GGJ 8, 27, 6–9)

Jesus also foresaw on the cross the false teaching of the "three persons of the Trinity" and was extremely displeased about this. In Matthew 7:9-11, He says:

⁹Or which one of you, if his son asks him for bread, will give him a stone? ¹⁰Or if he asks for a fish, will give him a serpent? ¹¹If you then, who are evil, know how to give good gifts to your children, how much more will your Father who is in heaven give good things to those who ask him!

These statements make it clear that Jesus will never give us His teachings in a way that is incomprehensible to us or which we will not be able to process spiritually, mentally, and intellectually. The Gospel texts become easier to understand if these terms are replaced. Here is an example, taken from John 14:8–11:

Whosoever sees the Son, sees also the Father
⁸Philip said to him, "Lord, show us the Father, and it is enough for us." ⁹Jesus said to him, "Have I been with you so long, and you still do not know me, Philip? Whoever has seen me has seen the Father (Love). How can you say, 'Show us the Father'? ¹⁰Do you not believe that I am in the Father (Love) and the Father (Love) is in me? The words that I say to you I do not speak on my own authority, but the Father (Love)who dwells in me does his works. ¹¹Believe me that I (Wisdom) am in the Father (Love) and the Father (Love) is in me (Wisdom), or else believe on account of the works (Holy Spirit) themselves.

On the issue of the Trinity, at the behest of Jesus, the soul of Robert Blum explains the nature of God to a deceased monk in the afterlife. Here is an excerpt from Lorber's *From Hell to Heaven*, a description of the developments in the afterlife experienced by Robert Blum, a revolutionary, from Vol. 1, Ch. 126, 1–2:

> Jesus the Crucified is the only God of all the heavens and over everything that fills the infinite space. He alone is the Creator of all things, of all angels, humans, animals, plants and all matter. He is the Father according to His eternal love, the eternal Son according to His wisdom and the Holy Spirit according to His infinite power, strength and effect. Turn to this Jesus in your heart truly and faithfully and love Him, Who loves and loved you so much that He took on human nature out of love for all people and allowed the bitterest death to come upon the body, so that eternal life was to be made possible for you and all people.

In his book *Die Irrtuemer der Religionen und Wissenschaften fuehren zur Selbstvernichtung der Menschheit* (*The Fallacies of Religion and Science Will Lead to the Self-Destruction Of Mankind*), Wilhelm Pfaffenzeller writes that the concept of the tri-theistic God was established as a creed by the pagan Emperor Constantine at the Council of Nicaea in 325 as a means of ending disputes among the Christians, which had already become intolerable at that time. Emperor Constantine stated:

> This demented squabbling among the priests is incomprehensible to me. Their disputes are based upon petty quibbles. But this much do I know: I will not allow these quarrelsome zealots to destroy the Empire.[2]

He did not want these disputes to weaken his empire, but instead, wished to make use of Christianity to consolidate his government, because he recognized the moral virtue and state-sustaining strength inherent in the Christian faith. In the words of the Nicene Creed, with its affirmation of the three persons of the "Trinity," rather than a single God with three attributes, all Christians are confronted with the influence this pagan ruler has had on our faith, even to this day. When the ruling powers and the Church fathers prevent their subjects from having direct access to the true God, this makes these people easier to exploit, i.e. to control and manipulate, since they will be unable to develop their own internalized and fixed value system and will instead be helplessly at the mercy of the prescribed dogma. Where there is no personal relationship to God, and in the absence of a value system, it is very difficult for God's seed to germinate into human understanding. Even Martin Luther found the concept of the Trinity dubious. In a sermon on Matthew 3:16–17 held on June 16, 1538, Luther stated:

> Trinitarianism is a very poor expression. In the Godhead exists supreme unity. Some may refer to it as the Trinity, but this sounds to me all too scornful. Augustine likewise laments that he has no adequate word [...] Call it a threefold. I cannot give it a name.[3]

In the New Revelation, God Himself gives an allegorical explanation of His essence: the image of fire and flame. The fire and the flame together represent all-embracing Love: the Father. The glowing light surrounding the flame represents the Word and the Truth: the Son. The radiating heat stands for Power and Will: the Holy Spirit. Fire and flame are ONE entity and not *three*, as is taught in the "three persons" of the Church's Trinity doctrine.

The Allegory:

Fire + Flame	**represent**	**Father + Love**
Light	**represents**	**Son + Word + Wisdom**
Warmth	**represents**	**Holy Spirit + Power + Will**

An especially impressive contemporary pictorial representation of God's essence can be found in the image of the "Merciful Jesus," as revealed in His appearance to the Catholic nun Faustyna Kowalska. Jesus (the Universal Love in whom we can trust) pulls open his garment over his heart and two rays of light emanate from it: one white (water: Soul, Truth, Word) and one red (blood: Warmth, Power, Holy Spirit). Every element of the painting is inextricably linked to its purpose and meaning. Jesus' face corresponds to the face of the Shroud. The spiritual content of the revelations given to Sister Faustyna – the overwhelming mercy of God – corresponds with the central message of the New Revelation. The title of Sister Faustyna's painting encourages, in addition to veneration of the image, a direct, personal, and individual trust in Jesus: "Jesus, I put my trust in you!" By means of the painting, believers can enter into direct contact with God, with no need for an intermediary. As Jesus related to Sister Faustyna:

> May even the most grievous of sinners put their hope in My mercy. They, above all others, have the right to trust in the depths of My mercy. My daughter, write of My mercy for these afflicted souls. Souls who call upon My mercy give Me joy. To such souls do I bestow more graces than they would even desire. I cannot punish the most egregious sinner; if he invokes My mercy, then, in My boundless and unfathomed mercy, will I justify him.[4]

God's incarnation as the Messiah provides all people, through direct contact with Jesus and in living according to his teachings, the opportunity to learn how to become Christian children of God. In an inner and personal conversation, God provides believers with their own individual explanations, help, and guidance, enabling them to then and live and act accordingly.

Jesus explained to Lorber that the true meaning of the words of the Lord's Supper "hoc est enim corpus meus" is to "first hear My Word (bread) and then act (love-deeds-wine):"

> Say I: "Indeed, for bread and flesh are one and the same, just as wine and blood are one and the same, and whoever eats the bread of the heavens through My Word and does according to the Word, that is, drinks the wine of life through the works of the true, most unselfish love for God and for the fellowman, also eats My flesh and drinks My blood. For just as the natural bread enjoyed by man is transformed in man's flesh and the wine drunk is transformed into blood, so in man's soul My Word is transformed into flesh and the wine of love into the blood of the soul." (GGJ 9, 73, 2)

The Eucharist, or Lord's Supper, is allegorical for the way in which Christian teachings serve to feed our souls and build up our eternal spiritual essence. In an open-minded spiritual examination of Christian teachings, the Lord is spiritually present.

To exist as children of God, it is very important that we recognize the three-layered nature of our own essence: we humans, too, are of a triune nature. We are made up of body, soul, and spirit. The Apostle Paul says in 1 Thessalonians 5:19: "Quench not the Spirit." And yet, since the Spirit was expropriated, so to speak, from human beings at the eighth ecumenical Council of Constantinople in 869, this is no longer observed or taught in the Western churches.

Human beings have "unam animam rationalem et intellectualem:" they possess a soul that is both rational and spiritual. But apart from this soul, they have nothing spiritual. Hence their triune essence – body, soul, and spirit – has been deprived of the spirit. As an outcome of the Fourth Council of Constantinople, it is still considered un-Christian today to speak in terms of body, soul, and spirit.

I believe that it is our task in life to cultivate the unique, divine spiritual spark that is within each of us by entering into contact with the Holy Spirit. In the afterlife, our purified and spiritualized souls will then form the body of our consummated spirit, just as here on Earth, our body serves as a house for our soul. In the New Revelation, Jesus uses the very descriptive term "soul-purifying machine" to describe the human body, the physical "instrument of perception" given to us by God.

The disavowal and denial of the existence of the divine spirit within humans is a result of the nonsensical separation of God's attributes into three persons. Without an accurate understanding of the nature of God, it will not possible to understand the nature of human beings (the children of God). Likewise, without an accurate understanding of the Spirit, it will be impossible to understand the act of the divine Spirit speaking directly to the human spirits of the prophets. Even today, in the teachings of most Christian churches, this serious error regarding the human spirit, which dates back to the first millennium, has not been rectified. Within the Western Church, this confusion of terms has, very sadly, thwarted God's intention to be a personally accessible and visible "Father" to each person.

I believe that Jesus had already foreseen this, because, as an expression of disapproval, his Shroud contains the visible symbol of "the frown wrought by thorns." Today, thanks to the knowledge revealed in the New Revelation and through our advanced technology, access to these signs, which were placed directly by God on the Shroud, is once again available to all humanity. The interpretation and acceptance of these signs could, through a personal and individual relationship with Jesus, lead Christianity to a spiritual resurrection.

During His teaching ministry, Jesus sought to explain His nature to the disciples. But prior to the Resurrection, the Son of Man had not yet become the transfigured garment of the Deity. Not having yet experi-

Figure 20: The "Merciful Jesus" by Sister Faustyna also represents this truth: Jesus (the Love in whom we can trust) pulls open his garment over his heart and two rays of light emanate from it: one white (Wisdom) and one red (Warmth, Power, Holy Spirit).[5]

enced the Holy Spirit and the events of Jesus' crucifixion, death, resurrection and ascension, the majority of His disciples were not able to fully comprehend the impending miracle and the significance it held. The difficulties the disciples encountered in understanding His incarnation and salvation are very clearly recognizable in the dialogues contained in the Gospel of John. John the Evangelist, however, provides the true explanation of the nature of God in his texts.

As a prophetic clue to the confusion that would arise from the concept of the "Trinity," God had Pontius Pilate write Jesus' name and title in three different languages on the inscription at the top of the cross. Three times, different words were used to denote the same thing. John 19:19–22:

[19]Pilate also wrote an inscription and put it on the cross. It read, "Jesus of Nazareth, the King of the Jews." [20]Many of the Jews read this inscription, for the place where Jesus was crucified was near the city, and it was written in Aramaic, in Latin, and

Figure 21: This painting by Matthias Gruenewald (1480-1528) is aesthetically very reminiscent of a flame. Christ Himself also uses the image of a flame to describe His essence. Stars can be seen in the painting's background and in the aureole.[6]

in Greek. [21]So the chief priests of the Jews said to Pilate, "Do not write, 'The King of the Jews,' but rather, 'This man said, I am King of the Jews.'" [22]Pilate answered, "What I have written I have written."

To emphasize the number "three" in his text, John also repeats the phrase "King of the Jews" three times.

In my opinion, the **Eastern Orthodox Church** does a better job of explaining God. There, the risen Christ is at the very heart of the community. The two most important icons of Orthodoxy are, first, the representation of the Mother of God in her mortal form, cradling the adult Jesus in her arms as though he were a child and gesturing to Him with her hand in a sense of salvation. The second of these icons is Christ as Pantocrator, the ruler of the world. This representation is the expression of the ETERNAL: Who was, and is, and will be. The Orthodox icons are worshipped with deep reverence. Artists strive to create replicas of the traditional icons that are as faithful to the original as possible.

Icons are viewed as also being "windows to Heaven." In the icon worship of the Eastern Orthodox faith, the image itself is not being worshipped, rather, the entity depicted in the image is spiritually present, while Heaven and the existence of the heavenly kingdom are portrayed. Throughout the ages, in the uninterrupted tradition of icon painting, Christian icons have continued to depict the image of Christ as He is portrayed on the Mandylion of Edessa, and this is reflected in the text for the consecration of icons. **According to tradition, this is what allows the icons to help believers establish direct contact with Christ.** These divergences from the Western religions may well have rendered reforms and bitter wars of faith within the history of Orthodox Christianity superfluous. This close personal relationship between believers and Christ likely also facilitated the resurrection of Christianity in Russia in the wake of the horror and sufferings experienced by the Church during the communist era.

I believe that the confused theological sophistries about the Trinity that the Church has adopted into its teachings have had the effect of making our salvation more difficult, even depriving us of it. It is therefore high time, after 1700 years, to correct this misconception and take seriously the sign of the 3 that Jesus left in His blood on the face of His human body. It is probable that one of the reasons behind the present erosion of faith and values is, as Jesus tells us, the false depiction of God in the "Trinity."

People no longer accept either this incomprehensible concept or an "obedient obligation to believe." For many people, the impossibility of understanding the beliefs being preached has led them to completely renounce religion. Our tri-theistic, Western Christianity is currently at risk due to this decline of values within our society.

The Symbol of the Cross and Its Portrayal in Ravenna

In addition to the symbol of the "three" formed out of drops of blood, the face from the Shroud should now be looked at in its entirety. When multiple photocopies with ever greater enlargements are made of the face, it becomes slightly distorted and a more lightly colored cross becomes quite clearly visible. Once this symbol is recognized as such, it often becomes recognizable on an undistorted image of the face as well. The cross is an ancient symbol. It appears in different forms in many of the world's cultures. When viewed in terms of its geometric components, the horizontal and vertical lines, it symbolizes the connection between Heaven and Earth. In Christianity, the vertical bar represents the relationship between God and humankind. The horizontal bar symbolizes the relationship between human beings.

> Jesus said:

> The cross, erected on your Earth, is in its summary a picture of faith. In its details, it represents with the upright bar, which is larger and longer than the crossbar, the love for God, and with the crossbar the love for the neighbor.[7]

As previously mentioned, in the original version of the New Revelation, Mayerhofer writes that Jesus gives us a very important explanation of the cross, which goes beyond the current prevailing symbolism: The cross is a fundamental geometric form present in the Creation and in all creatures. In *The Little Garden of the Passion*, No. 35, he writes:

> "My child, today My Word to you is to explain the cross, it is to make you feel and understand in the depths of the correspondences the real value and meaning, as it has never been revealed to mankind, the great mystery that lies in this sign. It is not without spiritual meaning that I was nailed "to the cross" and not condemned to another kind of death.

This form means – as can be seen materially – two directions which meet in one point, intersect there, and thus one „crosses" the other. One form, as an upright one striving upwards, is crossed by the other, which runs parallel with the ground, thus obstructing it. In the case of the One nailed to the cross, the head and heart are attached to the upright beam and the hands to the crosswise wooden beam; this means that the striving of the spirit and the soul should only be directed upwards, but it is interrupted by the actions, or the purpose of the former is "thwarted" by the latter. For the word "actions" actually only designates things and deeds that are carried out by hand, where the word is then also in the spiritual sense the soul's henchman, and serves it as means to an end. So here you have the spiritual equivalent for the form of the cross, which I chose by trying to tell my spirits in their language: „My aspiration to lead humanity upwards or at least a great part of humanity, was destroyed by wrong or opposite actions. During My earthly life, men too wanted to hinder My mission by their actions, only while on the pole up-wards My human heart stopped pulsating and My Head bowed, while My arms were materially condemned to inactivity, My Spirit escaped at the end of My mission, saying: 'it is done!' and My spiritual hands – free as they always were – rose as Wisdom asking Love with the words 'Lord! forgive them, because they know not what they do!'"

Elsewhere, Meyerhofer writes in *The Secrets of Creation*, in the chapter titled "The Symbol of the Cross in Creation":

And now I want to open still further to you other depths where exactly this cross as a symbol of My humiliation and glorification is either clearly represented or hidden in all forms of the created beings, and show you how even in the course of the worlds, in the form of their orbits and in the material and spiritual cosmic man this form always shines out; so that you may see that it was not insignificant in My way of life that I, the Creator of all that exists, had to suffer the bodily death just in this way, where, as with My birth, also the circumstances and places contributed to designate the descent of the Supreme Being, so also His going home in the manner in which it happened was worthy of the Creator of all beings and bore the stamp of divine qualities.

For you will have to consider well that the type of death by which I was to "breathe out My spirit" according to the concepts of men was not just the closest one, but that such a way of death had to be chosen, which for men should bear a sign of shame, but for Me it should bear **the sign of divinity** (emphasis in the original).

Further and more extensive explanations given us by Jesus regarding the symbol of the cross can be found in Mayerhofer's collected texts. **All or-**

Figure 22: Sun/Earth/Moon/Orbits/Ellipses with crosses (Peter Kutzki)

bits found in creation, in which moons orbit their planets, planets orbit their suns, or solar systems and galaxies revolve around one another, are egg-shaped or elliptical. The elliptical form can be graphically repre-sented by a cross with its two beams. Figure 22 illustrates this principle for the Earth.

Christ chose the cross as the instrument of His execution to symboli-cally portray His status as the incarnation of the Creator. If we imagine the orbits of the stars as being symbolized by crosses, then the starry sky ap-pears, spiritually, to be filled with "crosses," fulfilling the words of Matthew 24:30 in the inner consciousness of all people: "[...] the sign of the Son of Man will appear in the sky [...]."

Figure 23: Hubble Space Telescope/Light Crosses[8]

One rather humorous secular example of this truth, that the cross is embedded in round shapes, is illustrated by the history of the East Berlin Television Tower and its architecture. In the heart of Germany, which had been militarily defeated, divided, and occupied, the leadership of the "First Socialist-Atheist State on German Soil" built itself a landmark in East Berlin, in the form of an extremely tall television tower with a large spherical structure at the top, paneled in brilliantly reflective stainless steel. To the horror of the atheists, when the sun shone on the tower, a large cross of light was reflected, and they could find no way to prevent this phenomenon. On bright sunny days, the cross gleams unmistakably from this socialist landmark. The architects had not anticipated this optical phenomenon and it led to their fall from favor with the regime. Locals mockingly refer to this phenomenon as "the Pope's revenge."

In my research on symbolism and the symbol of the cross, I have until now only found Christ's interpretation, as given above, in the New Revelation and in the Ravenna mosaics.

In kinesiology, medications, food, objects, and beliefs are among the various things that are tested on the basis of muscle reactions. Through the muscle reaction test, the autonomic nervous system allows insight into the immaterial, emotional aspects of personality. In these tests, the unequal sides of the cross are considered to have a weakening effect and the cross has therefore been deemed to be negative. It goes without say-ing that the symbol of the highest possible cosmic dynamic could not be without effect on the nervous system and the soul. In the cur-

Figure 24: East Berlin Television Tower with reflected cross[9]

rent kinesiological view, only the inverse conclusion is lacking: If I am weak, this symbol will strengthen me. If kinesiology were to be applied more on a psychological and spiritual level, the potential effect of the symbol of the cross would be perceived in every aspect of our lives. It balances us and acts as an equilibrator. If I am weakened by something, this symbol can help strengthen me in my weakness. If I am too euphoric, it will weaken me, bring me back down to earth and set me back on the right path. In this way, the cross keeps us "in motion," with its balancing and stabilizing effect on our lives. A deeper exploration of these influences will perhaps be the topic for another book.

If, because it symbolizes the laws of motion of the orbits of the planets, moons, suns, and solar systems, the cross is an all-encompassing symbol for Creation, then the Crucifixion takes on a deep symbolic meaning that goes beyond the worldly: In the act of Jesus' Crucifixion, humans spread out the Creator on the cross, above His Creation, visible to His creatures in the form of the Son of God, Jesus. The cross symbolizes the Creation. The spreading of the Gospel, Jesus' messages about the universe, signifies the tasks of humankind and the work to be accomplished by children of God for eternity.

In pagan times, much of the power held by the priests was derived from the ignorance of the people about nature, the world, and the cosmos. The pagan priests used frightening natural phenomena like earthquakes, storms, droughts, or lunar and solar eclipses to compel their believers to make great sacrifices to appease the alleged "wrath of the gods." To ensure that truth prevailed over superstition and paganism, Jesus taught His disciples about the nature of the earth, the moon, the sun, and the universe. His apostles and disciples understood the nature of the universe.

In Ravenna, there are wondrously preserved mosaics that perfectly depict this knowledge possessed by the early Christians, as well as its symbolism. The first Bishop of Ravenna, Apollinare, is considered to have virtually been an Apostle. He was evidently extremely knowledgeable about the teachings and life of Jesus, and the Christian traditions have been well preserved in the artistic portrayals. More details about the artwork in Ravenna will be provided at a later point.

As a result of the iconoclasm (controversy surrounding religious imagery) that took place between 726 and 842 A.D., very few early Christian works of art escaped destruction or were preserved. This historical controversy within Byzantine theology regarding imagery arose from the accusation that icon worship was "iconolatry," an imitation of idolatry. The accusation was refuted when the controversy came to an end with the argument that the images were replicas of the original "not-made-by-human-hands" icon and thus imparted the spiritual presence of the person depicted. Nevertheless, these disputes over the icons, combined with the growing influence of Islam, meant that almost all of the ancient icons were destroyed. The marvelously preserved mosaics in Ravenna therefore represent unique examples of early Christian art.

Figure 25: The Mausoleum of Galla Placidia (Peter Kutzki)[10]

These mosaics were created not long after the time of Jesus' life and ministry. Three large crosses (not crucifixes) are portrayed in the middle of a starry sky.

The mausoleum of the Empress Galla Placidia (392–450 A.D.) can be regarded as the immortalization in stone of a teaching of Jesus on the unfolding of the Divine Spirit in humans. From the outside, the building appears quite unassuming, inconspicuous, and small (Fig. 25), but inside, its vaulted ceiling contains a wonderful portrayal of an infinitely vast starry sky with a golden cross at the center.

The artwork displayed in the apse at Sant'Apollinare in Classe near Ravenna[13] is a brilliant illustration of the fact that, through the process of allegory, images can be used to reveal spiritual content. Allegories must always be viewed in context and therefore have more than one interpretation. A plant, for example, is green and therefore full of hope. It grows and reaches for the light. If we look for the allegories in the apse, the entire history of Salvation is revealed. God fashioned His physical

Figure 26: The vaulted Mausoleum of Galla Placidia in Ravenna.
In the main vault, a golden cross is depicted in the middle of a starry sky, with the four Evangelists, who spread Jesus' message to every corner of the universe. Some of the 900 stars in the vault are displayed in concentric circles or in circular forms that spiral inward. The vault is an invaluable masterpiece of Byzantine mosaic art, dating from around the year 450 A.D.[11]

Creation to be capable of creating images in His likeness. Everything was set in place for the achievement of this ultimate goal.

From small beginnings (the stones), concepts develop (the grass, knowledge of mundane life, things we can perceive sensorily), followed by deeper understanding (bushes, simple knowledge), and finally, spiritual knowledge (trees that are reaching to the sky, inner awareness). The birds (spiritual feelings, emotional disposition) live happily among the branches. The souls (sheep) thrive in the natural environment. Apollinare is another example. Through diligence (the golden bees on his robe), he earned his place in Heaven (the halo). Another interpretation of bees could be that Apollinare's preaching was as sweet as honey. From the spiritual world, Christ influences the physical world (the separate

Figure 27: Apse in Sant'Apollinare in Classe[12]

medallion with starry sky, cross and Christ). All of this is under the hand (power and guidance) of God. Above the physical world rises the spiritual world, in which Jesus Christ is enthroned as ruler. The archangels support the universe (on the pillars of the vault). The souls that have gone on to the hereafter (ascending sheep above the arch) continue to move closer to God. Between Bethlehem and Jerusalem, Christ's life unfolds, forming the foundation for the re-creation of Heaven. This is a very brief overview of one possible interpretation.

Through their own reflections, observers can gain insight into the interconnections between this world and the universe. Likewise, even our everyday surroundings can be interpreted by us in terms of their relationship to God.

A third golden cross is found in the Archbishops' chapel in Ravenna. Here, too, the cross is situated in the middle of the starry sky.

Figure 28: Center of the Apse in Classe[13]

Figure 29: St. Apollinare in his Bishop's vestments[14]

The Portrayal of Christ's Peaceable Kingdom in Ravenna

In the apse of the Basilica of Sant'Apollinare in Classe, near Ravenna, a peaceable, rich, and idyllically beautiful world of early Christian imagery is displayed, in which we can see St. Apollinare dressed in a bishop's robe. St. Apollinare is closely associated, both spatially and chronologically, with the Apostles. According to some sources, he lived during the first century A.D. The overall design of the apse is a depiction of Christ's life on earth and a unique artistic representation of His transfiguration on Mount Tabor. Here, Christ is portrayed in a profoundly symbolic way, gazing out from the center of a cross, adorned with precious stones, in the middle of the starry sky. The outline of the starry sky is round, evoking the impression of a gate or window into the reality of the next world. This representation, unique in the world, powerfully symbolizes the divine nature of Jesus Christ (Fig. 27). The golden sky descends to the

Figure 30: Archbishops' Chapel with cross[15]

landscape, gently illuminating it in a way that signifies that Jesus Christ brought Heaven and Love to the Earth. Gold is a symbol for love. Moses and Elijah, the most important prophets of the Old Testament, appear in the golden sky as witnesses to the transfiguration of Jesus. The hand of God crowns the round apse. An image of Jesus as Pantocrator forms the upper end, surrounded, on the wall above the apse, by symbols representing His evangelists. Below Him on the wall, sheep are depicted, making their way toward Heaven. Both representations of the face of Jesus correspond to the face from the Shroud.

The apse in "San Vitale" in Ravenna portrays Christ sitting on the Earth's sphere between two angels and two people. This image can be viewed as an illustration of the Old Testament prophecy about the Messiah: "The powers of heaven [angels] will serve Him [the Messiah – author's note]."

The GGJ describes how the angels appear to help Jesus in His work with the people. When it came to the calling of His disciples, we read in John 1:51:

Figure 31: Apse in "San Vitale"[16]

> And He [Jesus] said to him, "Truly, truly, I say to you, you will see heaven opened, and the angels of God ascending and descending on the Son of Man."

The GGJ also tells us that the archangel Michael was incarnated as both Elijah and John the Baptist.

As an example, here is an excerpt from GGJ 9, 119, 2–10. Jesus says:

> So you are to see with your eyes the fulfillment of My Word, as it is written of Me: "And you will see angels ascending and descending between heaven and earth, and they will serve Him." [Here, Jesus was quoting the Old Testament.] First, I called Michael in the Spirit, who descended from the visible heaven to earth like a bright lightning bolt, so that all were terrified. But Michael stood before Me in all majesty, shining more brightly than the sun, and no one but Me could bear his shining light. But I said to him: "John, cloak yourself so that My friends may look at you, recognize you and speak to you!"

Then he covered himself and stood in awe and love before Me and said: "Behold brothers! This is the Lamb who takes away the sins of the world from you and opens the way to eternal life! Believe in Him and love Him above all; for He is the very beginning and the very end, the Alpha and the Omega, the first and the last, – apart from Him there is no God!" When the angel had uttered these words in a very sweet voice, he bowed deeply before Me and praised My name. Then also all the others fell down before Me and praised Me like the angel. I called them all to rise and said to them: "Remain in your natural state; for I am now a human being like you and am in you through your faith in Me and through your love for Me as you are in Me. Therefore remain in your natural state!" Then they all rose up and John went to his former disciples and discussed with them about things that will come after Me concerning the Jews and the people of the earth because of their unbelief, and he remained in the visible human form as John [the Baptist], recognizable to all, among us all day long.

I believe that the *Great Gospel of John* heralds the Second Coming of Christ. The Bible contains innumerable references to this. It speaks of how God will break into our history during an existential, human-induced global crisis. Almost unimaginably for us, the Supernatural will break into our reality – to save us, but also to judge us.

Acts 1:11: [...] This Jesus, who was taken up from you into heaven, will come in the same way as you saw him go into heaven."

There will be a visible return of a physical, concrete person: the coming in glory of the Child from the manger, the Friend of sinners, the Crucified, the Risen Lord, the Righteous Judge and the King of the Universe.

Luke 24:37–39: [37]But they were startled and frightened and thought they saw a spirit. [38]And He said to them, "Why are you troubled, and why do doubts arise in your hearts? [39]See My hands and My feet, that it is I Myself. Touch Me, and see. For a spirit does not have flesh and bones as you see that I have."

The revelatory writings in the New Revelation are messages of hope for the entire world: Heaven and its hosts will descend to the Earth, and God has a plan for the salvation of our souls and our planet. The Scriptures reveal in great detail how hopeful these proclamations are. These writings can greatly inspire believers' sense of the power and capabilities of God and Heaven and can provide much comfort in the face of the seemingly insurmountable problems threatening our planet. Unfortunately, the New Revelation has gone largely unnoticed. This is why I am striving to bring my findings regarding the messages of the Shroud into people's consciousness, as a reminder of this cornerstone of the earthly kingdom of peace.

Symbols Communicate Complex Concepts

In accordance with the Jewish calendar, Jews who look to the end-times would await the appearance of the Messiah in a torrent of blood and in bloody garments in the year 5777. In our calendar, this was the year 2017. The insights provided by the Shroud of Christ would allow these Jews to recognize their Messiah through the blood shed long ago. For instance, the "torrent of blood" from the side of the body and the "bloody garments" as well as the small trail of blood on Jesus' forehead in the shape of a "3," similar to a handwritten Hebrew letter "Zadi," are clearly identifiable. The "garments of the Messiah," in the form of the Shroud of the Dead and the Sudarium of Oviedo, are truly covered with blood.

If humanity were to be willing to return to the true teachings of God, it could perhaps be spared some of the hardships that will precede the return of Christ, which are also proclaimed in the Bible.

To repeat: it was not God, but humans, who demanded the cruel slaughter of Jesus, and God permitted this solely for the sake of free will. In GGJ, 8, 149, Jesus refers to His crucifixion, explaining:

> Behold what I have to say to you all: I do not want it to happen like this, and I would have means and ways to redeem and save My children even without what will happen. However, the evil people want it in that way. And that is why I allow it to happen in such a way so that exactly through this also many wicked may convert to repentance, penance, and to the true faith in me! Because the rabble in the temple says and cries it out in one go:
> "Let us seize and kill him! If he will rise again from the grave, we will believe in him, too!" They want to put Me to this final test and so it shall be permitted! Through this, many who are now still blind as a bat, will see and believe in Me, but the fundamentally evil will thereby fill the cup to the brim and sink into their judgment and eternal death. But you will be comforted and rejoice! When I have risen from the grave, then I will come to you and convince you of the truth of what I have now spoken to you.

The New Revelation gives us the following insight: the path that an individual chooses is left to his or her own free will. Either a voluntary path to God through love and knowledge or a path that leads to the furthest distance away from God. Outside the material world, in the hereafter, making a decision between these two extremes, with the consciousness it requires, is not as simple and straightforward for the soul as it is here in space and time on earth. This is where the New Revelation, in the "writings on the hereafter," provides deep insights into God's mercy and the soul's evolution in the hereafter. The scope of this book allows us to only touch upon these revelations. In GGJ 3, 177, 110, we read of the dignity of the freedom of the human will:

> I say: „Yes, listen My dearest one! This is a matter of the greatest necessity on that globe on which men are destined to become true children of God by their own effort! If I in the least limited man`s freest will, this would totally ruin My purpose! Therefore, on this earth man must always be given the widest scope for his development, either leading him into the lowest depravity far below the deepest hell, or to the highest virtue beyond all heavens; otherwise no one could attain to the sonship of God on this earth which is destined for this particular purpose. And therein lies the secret reason why even the most wonderful divine teaching is in the course of time trampled down into the dirtiest mud! No one will be able to say that My teaching demands anything unnatural, unfair or impossible. Yet in the course of time such many rigors and impossible to carry out adjuncts will be added which no man will be able to observe to their whole extent. There will be hundreds of thousands of people slaughtered in exaggerated zeal, worse than the wildest beasts of the forest, and they will think that they are doing God a most pleasant service. Yes, I Myself shall have to allow the people, if they wish it so, to capture Me and in the end even kill Me physically, in order to thereby give them the freest and fullest scope for the exercise of their will. For only out of this highest and completely unlimited freedom are then the people of this earth fully capable of rising to become the truest and in everything godlike children and themselves gods. Just as I Myself am God only through my completely unlimited will-power and might God from eternity to eternity, also the children of My love must become that for eternity! But in order to become this exactly that spiritual course of education is necessary, which so far you do not like at all. But just think a little bit about it and you will find that it cannot possibly be otherwise! Where the highest can be attained, the lowest must also be present!"

The different ways in which the Shroud has been interpreted and the changes these interpretations have undergone over the centuries exemplify for us that God's revelations and His word are "living." Individual comprehension of them changes according to the demands of the age and the expansion of human consciousness. The emblem we have received in the form of the Shroud of Christ is also "living," and the possible interpretations of it change to accommodate both individual insights and current findings from Shroud research.

In Christianity, Jesus' death on the cross has given the symbol of the cross special significance. In early Christian art, however, it was rarely portrayed, since it was generally considered to be a symbol of shame. Not until around the year 425 do we find the crucified Christ being depicted.

Far more frequently, the images were of a plain wooden cross, or the "Lamb of God" was portrayed on the cross in place of Jesus' body. In 692, a synod decreed that the human figure of Christ on the cross be substituted for the lamb. Early Christianity's depictions, as can be seen in the wonderfully vivid mosaics of Ravenna, did not yet include Christ crucified.

Images of the living "Pantocrator" and later, of the sovereign "Christ the King" on the cross were created during different artistic eras.

The great slackening of religious beliefs and the distortion of the meanings inherent in the profound inner understanding of Christianity can also be observed in changes to the ways in which Christ has been portrayed in Western art over the millennia. We see this in the fact that, on many modern "crucifixes" in contemporary Western churches, the depictions of the powerless, tortured, dead Christ on the cross have a horrifying deterrent effect. In my view, Christ's divinity has been "dishonored" in many artistic renderings by their focus on the human aspect of suffering. In recent centuries, this has resulted in a complete loss of knowledge in the West as to how Jesus truly appeared. Taking into account the cosmic interpretation of the cross as a symbol for the orbits of creation, the traditional depiction of Jesus as Pantocrator, ruling over the world or the universe, can also be seen as representing "Christ on the cross."

Figure 32: Image of the Shroud with artistically enhanced outlines of the symbols and other markings (Wolfgang Grimme)

Reflections of the Author on the Image on Figur 32

I, Jesus, am who I am, the Creator of the universe, the absolute Love, from which flows the Wisdom and Power of the universe. For my children, I am the visible threefold union of Father, Son, and Holy Spirit.

On my "testament," I have left for you the most important symbols of Christianity, so that you may recognize me. Behold, how immeasurably I love you. I desire that you small earthly beings be free, self-confident, and loving children. To this end, I took upon myself the terrible torment of My crucifixion by My enemies. Death could not destroy My being. By dying for you, I was able to transform the matter of My body back into light and energy and reveal immortality to you. If you so desire, the same will also be true upon your death. On the day of your death, you will be born as a soul-spirit-being in My spiritual kingdom. You are children of God. Because you are My child, I, your Father, want to draw you to Me throughout eternity. When you recognize and understand deep within you that you are an eternally living spirit being, then your sense of forsakenness in the cold, dark, and infinitely vast material universe and your fear of death will cease forever. You will discover the path to My kingdom of Love in My name and image, in My creation, and in My words. If you desire it and request it of Me, My Holy Spirit will provide you with the strength you need for the essential expansion of your consciousness and for what is good, even in the most difficult of times. In your hearts, the greatest of all miracles will take place: you will hear My word there; do not give up when faced with difficulties. I, your Creator and Father, also did not give up. My mortal body passed through the gates of Death for you and on this linen cloth I have left for you, as a signpost and emblem, the truth about My and your resurrection.

Descriptions of the Symbols on the Shroud

In what follows, I would like to present a summary of my visual and textual allegory-like interpretations of the markings that have until now been identified in the image of the photographic negative of the Shroud. These are intended to serve as inspiration for personal prayer or meditation. To make the symbols easier to identify, their contours have been graphically enhanced on the photographic negative of the Shroud. The outlines of the symbols have been darkened and the bright areas, where the blood collected, have been highlighted in white. In my experience, once the symbolic messages on the face of Jesus have been internalized, they immediately appear in the mind's eye when gazing at the Shroud.

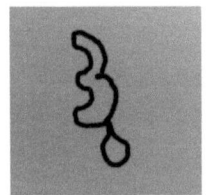

Figure 33:
The Trinity

The first thing that stands out is the number "three," drawn in blood, with the droplet hanging from it. Blood symbolizes the Spirit. Here, the Spirit of God has left a very brief testament on the face of Jesus, which can be read as being a gift to us in our day and age, with the resources we possess.

The formation of the blood drops surrounding the "3" on the forehead can also be interpreted as the Arabic numeral "1000" (see Fig. 8, page 41).

Jesus explains the meaning of the number "1000" in a revelation to Lorber (*Heavenly Gifts,* vol. 3, p. 367, "The Millennial Kingdom"): The digit "1" in the number 1000 represents Me in My human form; the three zeros following the "1" represent Me in the fullness of My divine Trinity.

Viewed this way, this formation duplicates and confirms the interpretation of the "3" as a symbol consciously created by Jesus.

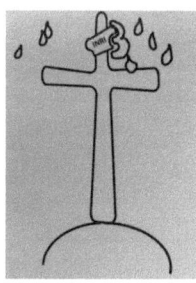

Figure 34:
Golgotha

One of my interpretations of the symbols on the Shroud shows that, in the center of the face, a cross with a plaque appears on an arch:

Golgotha!

Readers are free to form their own opinions about the self-explanatory symbols, which really do not require any further clarification.

Figure 35: Commonly used symbol for the Trinity

On the contrast-enhanced reproduction of the image, a triangle appears on the forehead, outlined by the drops of blood and the horizontal beam of the cross. The triangle is a commonly used symbol for the Trinity; the "three" appears as a name in the middle of the triangle.

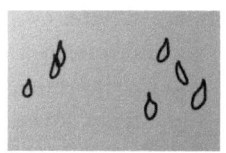

Figure 36: "The Seven Spirits of God"

On the forehead, we can see a triangular formation made up of seven very distinct drops of blood.

According to the New Revelation, the sacred number seven also symbolizes the seven spirits of God: **Love/Wisdom/Will of God/Order/Divine Earnest/Patience/Mercy.** These seven characteristics, or "spirits of God," are also mentioned and described in the Old Testament. The seven spirits of God are also the reason that we have seven days in a week. The period of rest that is prescribed for the seventh day (the Sabbath) is a spirit of Mercy, meant to "mellow out" our busy week.

Visually, the fourth, or middle, droplet, represents "Order," which has been placed at the bottom. Allegorically, this symbolizes the "fallen order" that compelled the incarnation of God. Through His human existence as Jesus, He personally guided His fallen creatures back into spiritual freedom, teaching them what they needed to know. Mayerhofer writes in "The Work," (*The Garden of Life* anthology, No. 43,1872):

> It is true that I had different intentions and purposes with the first man when I created him; but I created a man with free will, not a machine, and so I could not resist when man did not become what he was to become. The first test for this was the prohibition: "to eat the fruit of a certain tree [...]." This prohibition was the **test of obedience;** this was to be tested by men in themselves, perhaps to achieve in a small scale what the great spirit [Lucifer] did not succeed in doing in its entirety! **This error of disobedience is the original sin** that man has inherited from his ancestor, and which is still the most fundamental error of all men. All of them sin either against My laws or against the laws that coexistence imposes onto them. Disobedience is everywhere, in the hut as in the palace, in the material world as well as in the spiritual world.

In another example, the configuration of the seven candles on the Jewish menorah is also 3–1–3. The lights of the menorah are interpreted as well as representing the seven spirits of God. Jewish scholars liken the menorah to knowledge of God and the Torah, and the Torah calls the faithful to also light the menorah in their own hearts.

If we observe the seven drops on the forehead from left to right, as if reading them, these drops become smaller and their placement in front of the symbol of the number three becomes less orderly. On the other side of the "three," they become larger and more evenly arranged. Reading from left to right, as in Latin script, one possible interpretation could be: After Jesus' life on earth, the spirits of Divine Earnest, Patience, and Mercy will become more powerful and people's lives will move in a more orderly direction. Reading from right to left, as with the Hebrew Scriptures, the order is reversed. In Luke 19:41–44 we read:

> And when he drew near and saw the city, he wept over it, 42saying, "Would that you, even you, had known on this day the things that make for peace! But now they are hidden from your eyes. 43For the days will come upon you, when your enemies will set up a barricade around you and surround you and hem you in on every side 44and tear you down to the ground, you and your

children within you. And they will not leave one stone upon another in you, because you did not know the time of your visitation."

Here is what Jesus had to say about this Bible passage in Mayerhofer's *The Lord's Sermons*:

Already in the revelations about "The Spiritual Sun," you will find explained what it means: "And Jesus wept!"
There, you are shown that spiritually these words express the deepest sorrow of God, who brought for His children His whole Kingdom of Heaven to His children to their earth, even showed them in a visible form their Creator and Lord of all the universes, and how the blind, in spite of all that, did not recognize Him, the manifestation of supreme love, meekness and grace. They did to Him whatever despicable and painful things can happen to a man, and spurned His teaching, the teaching of love, reconciliation and forgiveness. It was this great blindness of the majority of His contemporaries which made great Creator, visibly embodied as Jesus, shed tears of sadness. He wept over the decadence of the capital of the Jewish people, foreseeing their total end as an independent nation, followed into the distant future by the contrary line of thinking this nation, once chosen by Me for the greatest destiny, has pursued to this very day. (Homily 35, The Lord's Grief Over Jerusalem)

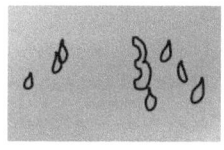

Figure 37: "The Number 10"

If we add up the seven drops and the "3," we arrive at ten: The Ten Commandments. Three commandments instruct us as to how we are to interact with God and seven commandments teach us how we are to interact with one other.

According to Paul Vignon, thirteen puncture wounds were the source of the blood flow that formed the markings on the face and temples. Around the symbol of the "3," there is a grouping of twelve additional bloodstains. Jesus had twelve apostles, and so, including Him, a total of thirteen people took up and spread His teachings at the dawn of Christianity. In this context, the number 13 can be seen as allegorical for Jesus and His disciples, a symbol of His ministry and the teachings He gave us.

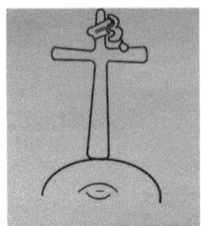

Figure 38: "The Word of God Remains on Earth"

In the arch under the cross (a symbol for the hill Golgotha or the earth) Jesus' mouth can be seen: Like a seed, His word remains on Earth, and this was the meaning and purpose of His coming to us humans. In Lorber's *Scripture Explanations* he writes:

I did not say, "He who will believe in Me, out of his loins will flow the rivers of living water," but I said, "He who will act according to My word will know whether My teaching is from God or from men!" (33, 16, pp. 165–166)

Since every human face is shaped according to the same principles as the face of Jesus, the symbol of the cross is also visible in the face of every human being. This serves to remind us that we should always look for the individual spark of God and the immortal soul within every one of our fellow human beings. Many other interpretations remain to be discovered in the course of time.

The Number 137

In studying the interconnections between religion and science, we came across the number "137." If the number one is divided by 137 (1/137), this results in the approximate decimal value referred to as *a* in the natural sciences. Alpha 0.007 297 373 ... is dimensionless and, in quantum physics, its value results in a physical fine-structure constant. Alpha is the quotient of 1:137.035 999 138 ...

Alpha's value was first determined in 1914 by the quantum physicist Arnold Sommerfeld (1868–1951), during his study of the hydrogen atomic spectrum. This constant links electromagnetism to the theory of relativity and quantum mechanics. It is regarded by physicists to be a "mysterious number." Many people have questioned what it might mean, but this mystery has not yet been solved.

According to the physicist Richard Feymann, the number 137 is something that all theoretical physicists should be wracking their brains over. He called it "one of the biggest damn mysteries of physics, a magical number that comes to us, that people don't understand. It's as if the 'hand of God' wrote this number, and we don't even know how he guided his pencil."[17] What I see in the number 137 is the number 1 for God, the 3 for His triune nature, and the 7 for the 7 spirits of God. This is a perfect abbreviation for God.[18]

Other Possible Interpretations of the Symbols

For those of the **Jewish faith,** the symbol of the three might most easily be interpreted as the modern, handwritten Hebrew letter "Tsahde." In some sources, the cabbalistic numerological interpretation of this letter includes the number 90, for the "fallen son." "Star, Aquarius, fishhook" are other possible interpretations. Does God set out a "fishhook" to catch the "stars" that became "fallen sons" during the age of Aquarius?

In GGJ 9, 116, 17–19, Jesus compares humans to fish. When asked why he would compare people to the most stupid of all animals, he gives the following explanation:

> You are probably not entirely wrong there; but still, for the most part, people are even more stupid than the fish in the water. If you want to make a rich catch of fish, do fish at night by the light of the torches; from this you will deduce – at least in the natural sense – that the fish are certainly not afraid of light, since they gather in large numbers at the place where they become aware of a light. I am the Light of all light and the Life of all life!
> But look at men, there is only a small number of those who swim towards Me in the water of their worldliness and let themselves be caught by Me into the kingdom of God! That is why I compare only those few men with the fish – who are my dearest food – who recognize Me as the true light of the world and as the sun of the heavens and swim towards me and let themselves be caught by Me to eternal life. – Do you understand this picture?

Would it be possible to interpret Jesus' frown as His response to the contemporary Jewish clergy's mockery of His task and mission as Messiah? Could it perhaps mean that the mind should not be glorified? Without the power of heart and love, the mind becomes a very arduous and thorny path to God. Or, can the involuntary frowning be seen as a symbol of humanity suffering under a "thorny dictatorship"?

The symbol vaguely resembles the letter "He" from the Paleo-Hebrew alphabet. This letter appears twice in the Hebrew name for God.

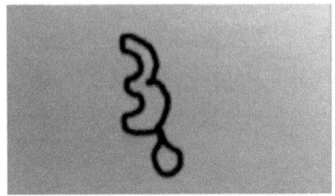 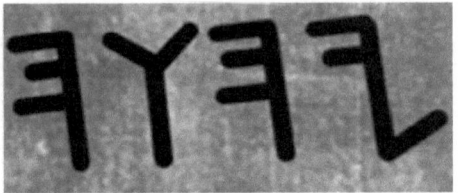

Figur 39: The name of God in Paleo-Hebrew script

According to the New Revelation, Jews, who are descendants of David, have, through their physical blood relationship with Jesus, a high spiritual calling as Christian prophets. Devout Jews who fail to accept the Messiah may be faced with a very painful awakening in the hereafter. Jesus discusses just this in a conversation with Cyrenius, the brother of Emperor Augustus, the Roman governor:

> But all this will not get lost,[19] and when there a thousand and not quite a thousand years will have passed from now on and My teaching will be almost completely buried in the filthiest matter, I shall at that time awaken men, who will write down word for word everything what has been negotiated here by you and by Me. They will present it to the world in a large book, and many will thereby have their eyes opened again. (GGJ 4, 112, 4)
>
> Also, most of the others with a great calling will be descendants of David. For such things can only be entrusted to those who even in the flesh descended from where I also descended in My flesh. Since Mary, My earthly mother, is a purest daughter of David, I also am a descendant of David. In those days, these descendants of David will be mostly be living in Europe, but nevertheless they will be very pure and genuine descendants of man according the heart of God and capable of bearing the strongest light out of the heavens. (Ibid., 8)

When asked whether the will of God would at all times only be revealed to the descendants of David, Jesus gives the following answer:

> Say I: "Friend, this does not happen here by the way of secret revelation, but by open word well audible to every physical ear! But it is a totally different matter to hear the secret inner word that comes from My heart into the heart of the one who hears it in himself. For this it is necessary to have a certain prepared line of men whose innermost being is capable of bearing the omnipotence of My word! For one iota of what is coming directly from Me would suffice to destroy and kill one unprepared. But once it has been written,

people of good will and intention may read it; and this will then not only will it not kill them, but strengthen them to eternal life." (Ibid., 10)

For thousands of years even the Jews were led astray and kept in the dark by their own priests for the sake of maintaining their rulers' positions of power and material sustenance.

If, within **Islam**, there were to be an acknowledgement of the "not made by human hands but by God" image of Jesus on the Shroud, this could bring about a very rapid change in their concept of God. Since the image was created by God Himself, it would not belong to the category of forbidden imagery. The Shroud does not contain any false depictions of God and does not require any corrections for it to fall outside the prohibition of pictorial representations of God. If Muslims were to learn about the "miracle of the Shroud" and God's intentions and approach with the Shroud, they would be able to understand the importance of Jesus, whom they know from the Koran as a prophet. The teachings that the Shroud confirms would enable them to see that the Christian God is a God of love, who expects devotion and humility from us humans. Since it was not God who demanded the Crucifixion, but evil non-believers, the question of whether God calls for acts of violence against other people could also be re-examined.

Love is incompatible with any form of violence. The reality that God provides us with revelations, whose interpretations change in accordance with the demands of the times and with human consciousness, could offer them a new approach to their beliefs and the significance of the prophets.

This would also make it possible to question the truth of Mohammed's "unchangeable final revelation of Allah" in the Koran. This assertion of the existence of a final prophet is what has led Mohammed's followers to be separated from the living Spirit of God and to maintain the traditions of his time, with the result that his followers are not open to new revelations.

On the Shroud, the Christian God reveals himself as **one** God, not three gods. The difference between Mohammed (human) and Jesus (God) is also demonstrated by the "Shroud revelations," since no such evidence exists of Mohammed. Those Muslims to whom Jesus has very distinctly appeared and who have subsequently converted to Christianity are able to compare what they have seen with Jesus' self-portrayal on the Shroud.

Figure 40: Comparison of the Om symbol with the "three" from the Shroud (Peter Kutzki)

Jehovah's Witnesses could use the Turin Shroud to verify the truth of the proclamation made by their theologians that "Jesus died on the stake and not on the cross." This evidence could provide them with an opportunity to assess the veracity and intent of the theological teachings they have received.

With respect to the **Eastern religions,** I do not believe it to be a coincidence that the symbol of the "three" on the Shroud bears a similarity to the symbol for Om. Among the Hindus, Jainas and Buddhists, the Om symbol represents the "sound of the sun," the transcendent primeval sound whose vibrations, according to Hindu thought, gave rise to the entire universe. It is the most exalted and all-embracing symbol in Hindu metaphysics and signifies the highest understanding of God, the formless Brahman, the impersonal World Soul. In Buddhism, the symbol and sound of Om signifies the presence of the Absolute.

Believers from other countries, with different languages and cultures, can also explore for themselves the symbolism and messages the Shroud may reveal to them.

DNA Findings from the Shroud and Mary's "Virginity"

In 1995, the Institute of Forensic Medicine at the University of Genoa became the first laboratory to examine a blood sample taken from the Shroud. The findings can be summed up as follows: It was a very old sample, containing damaged and fragmented DNA chains, which had possibly been contaminated by male and female DNA.

Other scientists have subsequently carried out similar studies with material collected at a later date. The blood had decomposed, making it quite difficult to analyze it. Only after considerable amplification[20] did it become apparent that the sample being tested was potentially contaminated, as both male and female alleles[21] were present.

American physicist F.J. Tipler, however, well-known for his collaboration with J.D. Barrow on *The Anthropic Cosmological Principle*, comes to an entirely different conclusion in his book *The Physics of Christianity*. He determined that there was no contamination whatsoever of the blood sample. The blood is from a man with two X chromosomes, where one of the X chromosomes has been transformed (broken) into an SRY chromosome. Tipler maintains that one out of every 20,000 males has this genetic characteristic.

With respect to the blood from the Shroud, however, Tipler suspects that this characteristic could be the result of a particular parthenogenesis[22], in which an SRY gene was added to the female X gene, or that a DNA fracture in the second X chromosome of the female genes resulted in the SRY chromosome. This would then produce a male. He writes that he has been able to interpret the results published by the Institute of Forensic Medicine in Genoa in 1995: They are typical characteristics of the DNA of a man born from a virgin birth, i.e. conceived without a male.

In the human female, eggs reside in the ovaries in a dormant phase. Prior to ovulation, the egg divides into two cells with a normal diploid (double) set of chromosomes and only then does it undergo further cell division resulting in a reduced haploid (halved) set of chromosomes. It is therefore conceivable that the "overshadowing" of the Holy Spirit was, in reality, only a very minimal intervention, and that the progression of the first cell division, during which the X chromosome was broken, in the absence of further cell division to reduce the number of chromosomes, could have led to fetal development. What is also very interesting with regard to the "overshadowing of the Holy Spirit" are studies from the field of biophoton research into the effects of light, especially UV light, on chromosomal stability.

Men with X SRY rather than XY sex chromosomes are sterile. This could put an end to the speculation about Jesus and Mary Magdalene having had children together.

Photogrammetric Representation of the Shroud

I would like to now describe the assumptions that can be made about the appearance of the traumatized etheric and astral body on the Shroud based on findings revealed through photogrammetry.[23]

With the help of modern photogrammetry, based on Giuseppe Enrie's first photographs of the Shroud in 1931 in conjunction with photographs by Giancarlo Durante, the International Institute for Advanced Studies of Space Representation Sciences in Palermo, Italy has reconstructed movement sequences for the body in the Shroud as well as various other objects. The Institute's findings contradict the previously known facts. It is particularly difficult to reconstruct the formation of the blood stains on the Shroud under the assumptions made. The researchers believe that Jesus was buried lying on his stomach, because the muscles of His back do not show any signs of flattening.

They maintain that He was wearing a loincloth at the time of burial, that the Sudarium of Oviedo was folded into a cushion under His forehead in the tomb, that the crown of thorns from His head was buried with Him, and that the nails from the Crucifixion were still in the wounds at the time of burial. The right hand can be observed in various positions. However, on the premise that these represent recorded traces of our Savior's etheric and astral body, severely traumatized by His execution, we can resolve these contradictions.

It is not customary in Jewish burial rites for the body to be laid on its stomach. The photogrammetric findings indicate that at the time the image was created, the body's weight had no effect on its back. It appears as though the body were suspended between the two halves of the fabric.

If gravitation and magnetism are elements of "the Will of God" that created and holds together the universe, as declared in both the Bible and the New Revelation, this finding can then be explained by the following statement:

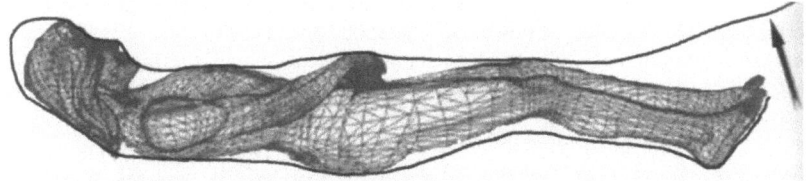

Figure 41: Possible configuration of the Shroud as the image of the body was created. The hypothetical excess pressure within the Shroud caused air to escape, which lifted the upper half of the Shroud at the body's feet.[24]

> On the third day of Passover, the Deity returned and called the body of the Son of Man, which forthwith completely dissolved and was added to the soul as a garment. (GGJ 11, 76, 1)

The center of the universe's gravity, God Himself, acted on the body lying in the grave and caused it to dissolve.

Viewed from this perspective, these current studies open up a very new, large, and broad field of research into the details of the Shroud, one that transcends our material plane and will require us to access the soul-spiritual levels of our existence.[25]

Another "Not-made-By-Human Hands" Image

Mary also left the world an image that was not created by human hands, or an "acheiropoieton:" the image of the Madonna of Guadalupe.

During the winter solstice of 1531, at a moment when the Aztec population was suffering from a collective depression, Mary appeared to them as a pregnant virgin, bringing Jesus Christ to the Aztecs. In the image she left during her apparition on the Tilma, the mantle belonging to the seer Juan Diego, Mary incorporated elements of the shattered Aztec culture. Standing in the aureole of the sun, she reveals to the Aztecs that Christ, whom she carries in her womb and who is symbolized by the "flower of the sun" (on the bow of the belt she wears to signalize her pregnancy), is the one true God. This representation, which was a type of codex for the Aztecs, had such an impact on them that they immedi-

Figure 42: Madonna of Guadalupe[26]

ately understood the message being given them. Within a very short space of time, this marvelous image led eight to nine million Aztecs to convert to Christianity. The apparition of the Mother of God heralded the birth of the Mexican people, because in the wake of this extraordinary event, the Aztecs and the Spaniards, who had been mortal enemies, united into a single nation.

The Guadalupe image has survived an accident involving acid as well as a bomb attack unscathed. The fact that the fabric, woven from agave fibers, has survived is a miracle that continues to this day, since these natural fibers typically decompose after a few decades. The dyes used in the image have not yet been able to be scientifically identified. In 1963, the Kodak company declared that the image bore characteristics of a photograph. Magnifications of the Madonna's eyes revealed a reflection of the people present at the time the image was created. As would be the case in the eyes of a living person, the image of the seer Juan Diego can be identified, along with other individuals.[27]

1   Brenske Gallery, Munich
2   Translation by C. Dyre.
3   Bayer, Oswald: *Martin Luthers Theologie: eine Vergegenwartigung.* Translation by C. Dyre.
4   Kowalska, Maria Faustyna: *Tagebuch der Schwester Maria Faustyna Kowalska aus der Kongregation der Muttergottes der Barmherzigkeit,* p. 351. Translation by C. Dyre
5   Painting of "The Merciful Jesus," by Adolf Hyla. The picture bears the words: "Jesus, I put my trust in You."
6   Painting by Matthias Grunewald (1480-1528) https://en.wikipedia.org/wiki/ Isenheim_Altarpiece#/media/File:Grunewald_-_christ.jpg (accessed 3 October 2020)
7   Lorber, *The Spiritual Sun,* Book 2, Chapter 48, paragraph 24.
8   https://en.wikipedia.org/wiki/Antennae_Galaxies (accessed Dec. 16, 2020)
9   https://en.wikipedia.org/wiki/Fernsehturm_Berlin (accessed Oct. 3, 2020)
10 Photo von Peter Kutzki.
11 https://commons.wikimedia.org/wiki/File:Galla_Placidia_Ravenna_06.JPG (acessed Oct. 3, 2020)
12 Berthold Werner, public domain, https://commons.wikimedia.org/wiki/File:Ravenna _BW_4.JPG (accessed 3 October 2020)
13 Ibid., detail
14 Ibid., detail

15 https://www.thebyzantinelegacy.com/archiepiscopal-ravenna (accessed Dec. 16, 2020)

16 https://commons.wikimedia.org/wiki/File:Ravenna_Basilica_of_San_Vitale_mosaic.jpg (accessed Oct. 3, 2020)

17 https://bigthink.com/surprising-science/why-the-number-137-is-one-of-the-greatest-mysteries-in-physics (accessed 6 November 2018)

18 For those who are interested in numerology, an interesting video can be found on YouTube: "3-D Hologram of Jesus. The Man in The Shroud" from "GoodShepard Film Productions," 14 July 2015, https://www.youtube.com/watch?v= tbqtxcoMNgY (accessed Nov. 9, 2018). The video presents information on items found on the Shroud of Turin that add up to the number 1128. Along with "Jesus of Nazareth," there is also "a number 3 seen in blood."

19 One of the explanations Jesus gave to his disciples that goes beyond the Gospels is found in GGJ 4, 112, 7: "One of those unto whom the greatest number of things will be revealed, more than unto all of you now, shall descend in the male lineage from Joseph's eldest son, and shall therefore also be a rightful descendant of David in the flesh."

20 duplication of DNA segments

21 components of chromosomes

22 asexual reproduction

23 Photogrammetry is a technique used to obtain 3-dimensional measurements utilizing photographs as the fundamental medium for measurement.

24 Giulio Fanti, *La Sindone*, p. 316.

25 YouTube: "Shroud A New Astonishing Phenomenon Discovered in This Find," https://www.youtube.com/watch?v=6wYtiKvzCmQ (accessed on Oct. 26, 2018)

26 https://en.wikipedia.org/wiki/Our_Lady_of_Guadalupe, public domain (accessed Oct. 3, 2020)

27 Also see the YouTube video: "The Shroud of Turin – Double Awakening" by Waldemar-Kurek-Mosakowski from May 19, 2017; Polish with English subtitles. The author has visually identified on the Shroud the face of Christ on the chest and the face of the Madonna of Guadalupe on the shoulder. https://www.youtube.com/watch?v=diE9QjdEsN8 (accessed on Nov. 9, 2018)

Summary

➤ God planned the Shroud, its creation and form as well as its temporal consequences for Christianity, and has carried out His plan over several millennia, up until today, so that He could provide us with invaluable inspiration. Well in advance of His earthly life and Crucifixion, God prepared the physical and spiritual messages that would appear on the Shroud,[1] something only God Himself could do.

➤ God incarnated as Jesus of Nazareth, was crucified, and rose from the grave as Christ. Without the Resurrection, there would be no image on the Shroud.

➤ With the transformation of the physical body into energy (light), God emblemized on the Shroud the reality of a non-material world and the existence of a realm beyond the comprehension of our five senses. It is an affirmation of the way He described Himself: "My kingdom is not of this world" (John 18:36).

➤ The Shroud of Turin is authentic; it is the Shroud of Christ. Since its creation, it and the power it holds within it have been with us, as a sacred emblem and a channel for contact with God.

➤ The Shroud of Turin has always been known as the "Shroud of Christ":
  – as a venerated object in Edessa
  – in its reproduction in the icons[2] of the Eastern Orthodox Church
  – in the direct worship of the Shroud in Constantinople, Lirey, Chambery and Turin.

➤ Within Christianity, the history of the Shroud has been seamlessly chronicled since its very creation. The image on it is evidence of the crucified Christ.

➤ The array of facts about the Crucifixion that emerge from the writings of the mystics did not become known in detail until scientific research began on the Shroud. The New Revelation, the Shroud research, and the interpretation of the symbols on the Shroud all mutually affirm each other.

➤ The complexity of the Shroud's creation and the slow, gradual development of scientific understanding over the ages make it impossible for its spiritual content to have been falsified. Only modern technology has made it possible to gain a deeper understanding of its meaning.

➤ The invention of photography permitted information about the Shroud of Christ to be disseminated worldwide. Photographer Secondo Pia recognized the visible face of Christ in a negative, which, in 1898, sparked a global sensation in the print media. At the dawn of the twentieth century, perceptibly at One with God, Christ brought Himself and His resurrection effectively and enduringly into human consciousness.

➤ To dispel any scientific doubts, Christ left self-explanatory symbols on His shroud that would speak to people's emotions. The allegorical symbols on His face are unmistakably intended for us in our day and age, as photography would not come into existence until 1,900 years later.

Once the image was reversed in a photographic negative, His features were first correctly displayed. Outlines and silhouettes on his face became distinctly visible. The markings of the "cross," "Trinity," "Golgotha," and "Menorah" as well as the traces of blood were made visible in numerical symbols.

The *"E"* in the furrows of his forehead now appeared as a **"3"** drawn in blood.

The resurrected Jesus Christ is the Triune God of Christianity and the "Om" of the Eastern religions. Furthermore, the curving trail of blood can also convey a symbolic sense of the following meaning: God = energy → E = 3 → Energy = God.

➤ There is no one God in three persons! The Trinity, as it is taught and depicted, is a massive misconception. It is certainly also no coincidence that the issue of the "Trinity" played an important role in Ravenna's history.

➤ In allegorical manner, the Shroud contains the most fundamental elements of Christian doctrine.

➤ The cross is a universal symbol for the laws of creation and reveals itself in such phenomena as the paths and shapes of the cosmic bodies. Simply gazing at the symbol itself provides balancing and supporting energy.

➤ At the same time that photography was coming into being, other new sciences were also emerging. It was the beginning of a period of

Figure 43: Photograph of the Shroud and its negative; photos by G. Enrie
(1931)
Side-by-side representation of the halved images of the face from the original fabric and the photographic negative illustrate the associations between
"E = 3" and "Energy is God" as well as "God is Energy" (both images pro-
cessed and divided by Peter Kutzki).

groundbreaking research in all of the natural sciences. For example, quantum theory brought about a paradigm shift in the field of physics. Research into questions related to energy, matter, and light ushered in the atomic age.

➤ The Shroud also represents a scientific gospel, which can be read with the help of scientific instruments and methods. For example, the DNA findings from the blood on the Shroud confirm Mary's virginity. An explanation for the as yet unclarified origin of the image on the Shroud could potentially be found in the field of quantum mechanics.

➤ The purpose and task of the prophets was, and remains, to supplement the traditional teachings of the Christian faith with their revelations, so that it would become easier for us humans to understand.

➤ Many of the scientific predictions made by Jakob Lorber, who referred to himself as "God's scribe," have been confirmed by later scientific findings. This documented evidence provides us with a sound basis for trusting in the truth of his spiritual prophecies.

➤ In *The Lord's Sermons*, the New Revelation also tells us that it is in accordance with God's will that scientists responsibly engage with religion and, in particular, encourage a sense of collective love among their fellow human beings. If they, through the purposeful power of their own free will, will practice compassion, this would benefit all people everywhere. It would enable them to discover and deepen their faith in the Triune Creator and lovingly establish their own personal contact with the Holy Spirit of God.

➤ The emotional and spiritual power of the Shroud has not diminished over the centuries. The world' s rulers and disbelieving powers do everything they can to make it seem false and counterfeit. Yet, occurrences of conscious communication with Jesus confirm that the image on the Shroud of Turin can mediate contact with Christ as the living God. It has a compelling and strongly supportive power.

➤ The mosaics found in Ravenna are an authentic representation of early Christian art.

---

1   see also Jesus' letter to Abgarus
2   Icons: windows to the spiritual realm

A Message from the Co-Author

In this section, I would like to it as vividly as possible share my thoughts about this book and the experience of writing it. This is because, every now and again, odd things happened. For instance, something that occurred one day while I was researching quotations for our manuscript. Suddenly, what I was experiencing in the present fused strangely intensely with my past. In the blink of an eye, some of the ideas I had had in my youth sprang to my mind. The emotions that this evoked in me allowed my youthful contemplative worldview, held during the springtime of my life, to blossom once again.

Even my work on the manuscript and the illustrations of the Shroud's markings stirred up symbolic references within me, sparking mental images and new understanding. And I also was given answers to questions that had long puzzled me. In other words, I found explanations for things that I had already assumed, which is why I do not believe that these affirmations were coincidental. Provided with many clues, I finally understood processes, similar to synchronicity.[1] No effect, which, according to the principle of causality, can actually only be produced by one cause, can logically be explained on the basis of synchronicity. One example of this is when you think of someone with whom you have not had contact for many years, and the person contacts you precisely at that moment.

This event could be explained away as a coincidence. But what if these kinds of coincidences are happening frequently, one after the other? It must, however, also be noted that all of my unresolved questions had stimulated my thinking, so I was naturally open to receiving such messages. Having had these experiences, I believe that divine help does not have to come to us instantaneously – in other words, not necessarily as we contemplate the image of Christ on the Shroud.

Often, just a few hours after reworking sections of the manuscript, but sometimes only after days of inner dialogue, I would receive information without having consciously or directly searched for it. I believe that here too, the time factor is not significant. This kind of occurrence can best be explained through the experience of a great researcher. Max Planck said:

For the religious person, God's existence is immediate and primary. From Him, from His almighty will, springs forth all life and all that occurs in both the physical and the spiritual realms. Even if our intellect cannot perceive Him, He can be directly comprehended through the contemplation of religious symbols and will impart His sacred messages to the souls of those who faithfully entrust themselves to Him.[2]

My Evolution

My personal religious experience began with my baptism, which my parents desired for me. During the course of my life, from my own wedding to the baptism of my son, I received all of the sacraments the Church is happy to provide in exchange for the money it receives from our taxes.[3] As a child, I dutifully accompanied my father to church on Sundays and holidays. Although very few of the faithful could comprehend the words of the highly educated clergy, worship services were always very well attended. My attitudes toward religion were shaped by the education I received in my schools and from my religion teachers.[5] Later in life, my own, more expanded view was influenced by my immediate surroundings and the media.

After almost half a century, my wife and I withdrew from membership in the Church without specifying the reason. This did not mean, however, that I had renounced my faith or my personal belief in God.

As a young man, I was interested in all of the various scientific reports being published at the time. Photos of the night sky and images of the universe particularly fascinated me. I had a passion for fantastical paintings and illustrations of the galaxies. I was also intrigued by mysterious black and white photographs, probably taken from Earth with 1950s-vintage telescopes. And I was extremely interested in scientific topics of the time in the areas of physics, biology and medicine. When I was about seventeen, I would often spend time poring over illustrations of the human brain that had been printed in a particular anatomy textbook. Although I had to use a German-Latin dictionary to translate the Latin names from the illustrations, I spent hours immersed in this book.[6] I enthusiastically drew my own pictures of the things that made an impression on me at the time. Even after half a century, I still fondly remember my small drawings, done in ink and colored pencil. Unfortunately, at some point, I got rid of them, which I now somewhat regret. I am glad that I at least kept some of my books from that time. When I leaf through the yellowed pages, the feelings that rise up in me touch my soul nearly the same way they did back then. It isn't a recollection of a specific situation or feeling, but that of an entire period in my life. The fact that most of us generally recall the

Figure 44: The elliptical galaxy NGC 51284[4]

beautiful and predominately good things from the past is also a feature of the brilliance of Creation.

It was perhaps ten years later, around the mid-1970s, that I came across images of strangely shaped galaxies in a book in the series "Aktuelles Wissen" (*Current Science*), edited at that time by Ruediger Proske. These black-and-white forms, existing far out in the universe, seemed to me to be similar in shape to my own drawings of the human brain.

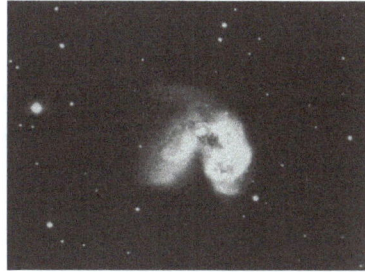

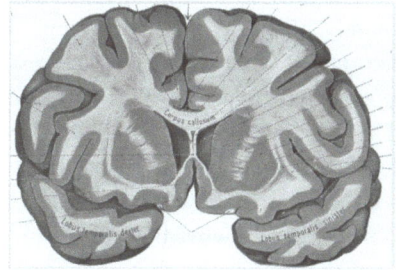

Figure 45: The spiral galaxies NGC 4038 and NGC 4039 are located in the Corvus constellation.[7]

Figure 46: Drawing of a human brain, anterior view[8]

The double galaxy system NGC 4038/39 is located in the Corvus constellation and consists of two closely spaced spiral galaxies, which also form a strong source of cosmic radiation.

The elliptical galaxy NGC 5128 is also known as Centaurus A, a powerful source of radio waves. The radio emitting lobes are arranged almost symmetrically on each side (like halves of the brain).

The shape and contours of the double galaxy pictured in Fig. 48 reminded me of my cross-section drawings of the two halves of the brain. Lateral views of our mental apparatus also look very similar to some of these formations. At about that time, it occurred to me that no matter how the universe may have been constructed or designed, it was possible that it consisted of an organized, orderly structure. During this phase of my life, my initial hypothesized worldview emerged in euphoric manner. This hypothesis opened up the possibility that there might be thought-capable galaxies in space. In my imagination, powerful energies and well-ordered formations in the universe might make it possible for consciousness to develop. It seemed to me that a sufficient number of the conditions required for this complex prospect existed in the cosmos. At the same time, I never had the feeling that I needed to continue to convince myself that there were any additional theoretical possibilities. That is because, for one thing, this imaginative view seemed to me to be more viable than any religious explanation I had encountered during my school days.

On the other hand, I certainly knew that I did not have a single piece of evidence that could prove the accuracy of my hypothesis. But ultimately, this was my worldview, my view of all of existence, in other words, my own religion. These exciting thoughts led me to believe that not everything in the world around us requires an objective justification. This is what I wanted to believe, and I could accept it in this intellectual form, completely free from any external pressure. In those days, there were only a few friends with whom I spoke about such thoughts. As I pondered the "why" behind the creation of human beings, I also considered the possibility that extraterrestrial monster aliens were playing an evil game with us. This alternative, however, did not fit into the picture for many reasons, not least of which was the insurmountable distance to the nearest planet. All the same, my rather audacious hypothesis gradually evolved, if only for me, into a vivid and purposeful worldview. In any event, there was no one at that time who could offer me a more suitable theoretical model. It was clear to me that a powerful, creative consciousness in the universe had meticulously planned the creation of all that lived and flourished on our earth. Over the years, nothing happened that might change this view. Not even when I repeatedly asked myself the question of the "why." I contemplated what the rational intention of such a powerful divine being would be, in creating countless galaxies with billions of solar systems. Why create planets like the Earth with its moon or the other celestial bodies? Why make the Earth the way it is, with its flora and fauna and creatures that live in water as well as on the land? Of course, I was always imagining a powerful spirit being, the great Id-Consciousness, who had the ability to create all the conditions necessary for this. However, in my thoughts, this was a being which, due to its unimaginable magnitude, would find it pointless to manifest itself physically for us in its entirety. I believed that even if this were to happen, it would be in a state that we would still not be able to comprehend.

Thanks to scientific illustrations, we have long had the ability to see in detail how the brains of living creatures are created. Instruments and techniques have also been developed that reveal the depth and form of the universe. Nevertheless, science has still not been able to provide comprehensible, conclusive explanations for many phenomena, which is especially the case when it comes to the phenomenon of "consciousness."

Once my thoughts had progressed to this point, I wanted to learn what had become of all the galaxies from that time. By entering the names that had already been assigned, I was able to find beautiful, new color photographs of them on the Internet. The two NASA images taken by the Hubble telescope show them in all their splendor.

Over the years, I held to my subjective explanations, even if the arguments that supported them were plausible only to me. The idea of a galactic consciousness correlated with my mental image of God. As a young person, I thought I understood that for such a powerful spirit, the dimensions of the universe and the duration of time would be of no importance. I used to believe that this divine being might feel lonely in the vastness of the universe, which, of course, due to its eternal nature, made no sense. But it is perhaps possible to conceive of these beliefs as wishes, as tangible fulfillment of desires? For it may be that children's firm belief

Figure 47: NGC 4038/39[9]   Figure 48: NGC 51285[10]

in the benevolent nature of their Father and their adoring and grateful recognition of His magnificent Creation is the source of their happiness and joy. Such lovingly induced feelings of happiness, multiplied by the great multitudes of good people, should be rewarding, even to a powerful Creator. This natural spiritual experience is best explained by the feeling of love that is reciprocated. Because I myself know what it means to me to feel loved, this alone provides me with an almost complete answer to my question as to the "why." This, together with the gift of free will, gave me and still gives me the conclusive reasoning for my views.

At that same time, I also became familiar with Albert Einstein's theories, which only belatedly allowed me to realize that, from a mathematical point of view, neither space nor time can be grasped as an absolute quantity. Conversely, it is difficult to comprehend why these fluctuating variables have been included as units of measurement in calculations in quantum or relativity theory. Despite the fact that the results produce conditions of space, time, and matter that scientists find difficult to explain, the speed of light, for example, has been determined to be the natural constant "C," which, in Einstein's famous formula, is squared. Natural scientists describe these research results as valid laws of nature. In his book *Secrets of Life*, Mayerhofer raises a justified objection to this:

"For them there exists no God, no lawgiver, although they presume natural laws; for them, it is 'substance,' which makes its own laws, thus an intelligent substance!"[11]

I could go on and further elaborate on my views on life and our human existence, but what I have said so far should give you a brief summary of my worldview and my personal belief system. For years, I was unaware that the even the most brilliant scientific discoveries and analyses and the insights they provide can only ever reveal minute fragments of the all-encompassing reality. I would like to add a quote from Albert Einstein, which to a certain degree affirms my ideas about God and the world:

"Everyone who is seriously involved in the pursuit of science becomes convinced that a spirit is manifest in the laws of the Universe–a spirit vastly superior to that of man, and one in the face of which we with our modest powers must feel humble."[12]

Matter Does Not Exist

From working on the manuscript for this book and through many conversations with its author, I learned that in the gospels written by Lorber, the mystic, there are several passages in his prophecies in which he also reveals special characteristics of the Earth's nature. One of the more peculiar prophecies states that matter, as materialists understand it, actually does not exist. Lorber thus wrote at several points in his books that matter does not exist; what humans perceive as matter is actually solidified spirit.

Some examples:

Thus, all matter was originally spiritual which of its own free will stepped out of God`s order, established itself within the wrong conceptions and, thus, became solidified; and this is what then formed matter, which is, therefore, nothing else but a judged and out of itself solidified spiritual; more precisely, it is a coarsest and heaviest encasement of the spiritual. (GGJ 4, 103, 4)

Said I: "Could anyone exist with his body on an earth that would not consist of all matter and its elements? Yet what are all matter and its elements? It is spiritual, judged and fixed by the omnipotence of God, but with the inherent ability advance to an ever freer to live an ever freer and thus more independent life!" (GEJ 9, 102, 1)

All primordial matter is fixed spiritual substance, and as it becomes free it also becomes active in its own way and forms its form and its nature with constant influence and effect of a corresponding spirit from the other side. We want to call this spirit positive-electromagnetic and add the name sideral spirit to it; we want to call the negative-electromagnetic substance or the directed earthbound natural spirit, which is primarily awakened by its corresponding otherworldly sideral spirit and is put into the activity corresponding to its inherent intelligence.[13]

Mayerhofer, too, in his *Secrets of Life*, states in several passages that matter is in fact not material at all, but merely the result of a spiritual fusion.

"As I have explained to you in earlier messages, 'body' was always identical with 'matter,' and I showed you that also in matter there is really nothing material, but only bound Spiritual. Or I told you that matter constitutes My fixed thoughts and ideas which remain matter or body as long as I do not withdraw My thoughts and ideas enclosed and embodied in the same."[14]

These and similar passages in the New Revelation seemed questionable to me at first. They consequently became typical sticking points in my discussions with the author. I asked her not to include these lines in the manuscript. I was afraid that chapters like these might have a negative impact on the credibility of the Shroud messages.

But just a few days later, almost coincidentally, the moment arrived in which my doubts were dispelled. It suddenly became clear that there was some particularly interesting scientific data that I had previously not been aware of. Although I knew that the field of modern physics had been around for more than a century, I, like most people, was not familiar with the details of the intensive research being done into quantum and relativity theory. I was browsing through some of the books from Gisela's secondary literature on the New Revelation and had glanced through their tables of contents, when I came across a brochure that had been published by the Lorber Society in 1990, as the Society was celebrating the 150th anniversary of Jakob Lorber's calling. A tribute printed in it described a speech given by the father of quantum theory, Max Planck. Because this short publication contained an abridged version of the Planck speech, I searched the Internet for the original version and found one:

Gentlemen, as a physicist who has devoted his entire life to the sober pursuit of science, the study of matter, there is no doubt that I am beyond suspicion of being taken for a religious fanatic. And so, after all of my research into the atom, I will say this: Matter as such does not exist.

All matter is created by and exists only through a force that causes the atomic particles to oscillate and that binds them together to form the tiniest solar system in the universe. However, since there is neither an intelligent nor an eternal force in the entire universe – mankind has not yet succeeded in inventing the much longed-for perpetual motion machine – we must assume that behind this force there is a consciously intelligent spirit. This spirit is the source of all matter. It is not the visible yet transient matter that is real, true, and genuine – **for without spirit, there would be no matter at all** – but rather it is the invisible, immortal spirit that is real! Since spirit as such likewise cannot exist, but instead, every spirit is contained within a being, we must necessarily assume that there are spirit beings. But, since spirit beings cannot bring themselves into existence either, but must be created, I do not hesitate to refer to this mysterious Creator in the same way that all the cultures of the earth throughout the millennia have named Him: God! And so, the physicist, who must concern himself with matter, proceeds from the realm of matter into the realm of spirit. And this is where our work ends, and we must entrust our research into the hands of the philosophers.[15]

Others among the renowned physicists who contributed to quantum theory in the early days described views similar to Planck's in their observations on matter and spirit. Even if such avowals are now rarely heard from within scientific circles, there have always been researchers, including Nobel Prize laureates, who straightforwardly shared their worldviews, their faith, and their religious beliefs with the world.

Against the backdrop of this book, which serves a guide through the signposts and symbols of German mysticism to the revelatory messages of the Shroud of Turin, I was particularly impressed by these quotations from Albert Einstein:

How can cosmic religious feeling be communicated from one person to another, if it can give rise to no definite notion of a God and no theology? In my view, it is the most important function of art and science to awaken this feeling and keep it alive in those who are receptive to it.[16]

Science without religion is lame, religion without science is blind.[17]

One fascinating scientist was the late Hans-Peter Duerr (October 7, 1929 – May 18, 2014), who served as director of the Werner Heisenberg Institute for Physics at the Max Planck Institute in Munich. Immediately after reading the speech above, I remembered that I actually owned one of Duerr's books, which had been in my possession for several years. His book, *Physik und Transzendenz. Die grossen Physiker unseres Jahrhunderts ueber ihre Begegnung mit dem Wunderbaren* ("Physics and Transcendence. The Great Physicists of Our Century On Their Encounters with The Miraculous") contains an essay written by Max Planck, entitled "Religion and Science." The book does not explicitly deal with quantum theory, so it is an especially rewarding read. It piques the reader's curiosity and, among other things, makes it clear that physicists had already reached the limits of explainability back in the 19th century. The fathers of modern physics, including Max Planck, Werner Heisenberg, Albert Einstein, Niels Bohr, Wolfgang Pauli, Erwin Schroedinger, Carl Friedrich von Weizsaecker and others, contributed essays to the book in which they transcended the dualism of "thinking and being," – in other words, spirit and matter. I knew I absolutely had to reread this book.

I had already read through a few chapters at the time I became interested in quantum theory. But at the time I bought the book, I simply didn't have the necessary powers of concentration. Now, my reasons for re-reading the book were completely different. It was my curiosity that prompted me to more thoroughly explore the encounters mentioned in the book's subtitle. Of course, I hoped that this exploration would lead me to discover as much as possible about "the encounters with the miraculous" experienced by these physicists.

I noted that strikingly often, the theoretical explanations the physicists provided fairly explicitly described the existence of a Creator Spirit, or even of a personal God. Unfortunately, however, in the final analysis, what is implied does not explain what may not be! Instead, it leads to clever reasoning all around the subject, since the task of the scientific community is to objectively examine "what is" – whereas it would be the task of the religious community to show "what should be." How then, I wondered, can religion credibly explain why things must be just so and not otherwise, if the most important condition for this is not stated? What happens if a prerequisite is suppressed or denied? Indeed, I could not remember any useful information that might have come out in the many years before I began this new quest that could have "objectively" revealed to me what "effectively" binds the world together at its core. Possibly, at least this is one way to understand it, because important principles of causality were abandoned early on, there can always only be calculated probabilities? Albert Einstein voiced his famous opinion on this, by simply and clearly stating that God does not throw dice!

In my opinion, the demand for new vocabulary is another difficulty. It has been said that with the words of our everyday language, it is not possible to accurately describe how and through what means the material objects of the world become visible to us. The author gave me a noteworthy answer to this question: "Where researchers search for a new language, mystics found it long ago. However, they must speak about God!" I cannot think of a more fitting argument in this context.

To my way of thinking, the dearth of language the scientific community possesses for such things as ascribing *an effect without any recognizable cause*, basically confirms the immediacy of a Creator Spirit. Even the incredible and unimaginably powerful energy and the colossal mass of matter in the universe is met with a kind of meek acknowledgement. Despite this, scientists find it better not to mention the Creator theory in public; it could harm their reputations. It seemed to me that the renewed enigmas of energy and matter in the micro- and macrocosm should not present a problem. If necessary, new mathematical tools could reduce these to useful probabilities. Similar to the way the Big Bang theory was constructed, assumptions and hypothetical elements may have to be employed to determine cause and timing prior to the tremendous act of Creation. However, researchers instead usually become quite prickly over similar explanations for the cause-less, time-less, eternally existing Creator.

I don't at all mean to suggest that all scientists are lacking this kind of language. The two preceding paragraphs are admittedly the result of the one-sided outlook I had taken on science in general until that point. However, my approach of painting everyone with the same brush was short-lived. There are and have always been researchers who are proficient in this challenging language. At the very least, they can cogently and intelligibly explain why it is so difficult for the scientific community to come up with new terms. They are also able to break down the problem of the "cause" in causality in a way that is readily understood and, by applying the calculus of probability, to clarify it, making it transparent and acceptable. And so, it was precisely these types of people we were hoping to find. One researcher in particular who, in his wise way of looking at things, was able to enlighten us about far more than just the linguistic difficulties in the field of science. The fact that this wisdom could actually be seamlessly incorporated into the topics presented in our book is something we consider to be divine providence. In any case, I consider it a wonderful achievement, because it allows the thoughts of a brilliant mind to be interlinked with the topics of our book.

Unfortunately, in my youth and during the course of my busy life, I never had the opportunity to read the New Revelations. I did not even know that these writings existed. Consequently, I missed out on the special insights that Christian mysticism provides. I was also forced to recognize that I had major shortcomings in my knowledge of the findings of the brilliant physicists of our German homeland.

God's New Revelation, as recorded by his faithful prophets Jakob Lorber, Gottfried Mayerhofer and Leopold Engel, and its connection with the epochal insights of modern physics might have motivated me much earlier to question my own religious worldview.

Looking back, however, I am somewhat reassured in this respect, because Max Planck once publicly stated that, to his sorrow, he had spent fifty years researching something that actually did not exist!

Basilica di Sant'Apollinare in Classe

The summer of 2018 was beautiful, and so we decided to re-visit Italy for a few weeks. We both wanted to again enjoy the wonderfully contemplative atmosphere of the magnificent buildings in Ravenna. The absolutely stunning mosaics, created from countless, colorful, gleaming stones, are fascinating. They are masterfully arranged in combination with gold-coated glass pieces on the ceilings and walls to form lustrous oversized images. In these churches, especially in the Basilica in Classe, the remarkably subtle feelings these masterly mosaics inspire are simply enthralling. Perhaps the peace that comes over us in these old houses of worship is due to the fact that virtually none of these magnificent works of art from the sixth century attempts to depict the unspeakable suffering of Christ on the cross. Apparently, the artists of that time felt that the injustice that human beings had perpetrated was too shameful to depict.

Figure 49: Basilica di Sant'Apollinare in Classe[18]

The Shroud's Message

Dear reader, perhaps you are also among those people who have already given some thought to what the reason might be for the existence and deeper significance of the Shroud of Christ, which has been with us for 2000 years. The author, Gisela Heinz, has devoted half of her life to answering and clarifying these kinds of questions. The way she presents her information on the Shroud and its spiritual messages is unique and extraordinary in comparison to the other Shroud literature that has been published to date. The fact that symbolic messages can be found on the Shroud in the image of Christ is one of the phenomena presented in the book. The marks that can be identified on the Shroud in the image of Jesus Christ can be understood as symbolic references. Even more, these symbols can appear as personal messages for each and every individual.

Being able to recognize identifiable symbols on the Shroud and understand their meaning as your own personal message is wonderfully simple, because it truly always works. You just have to trust and have confidence in God's power and love. Ideally, your entire heart and soul are involved in this. It doesn't matter whether you do this by thinking aloud, praying quietly, or meditating. What is most important is your sincere desire to connect lovingly with the Holy Spirit. Communicating with God is a very special experience. It is even more remarkable than might be imagined, because He generally accepts our requests and concerns almost immediately.

This still does not answer the questions we asked at the beginning: Why does the ancient Shroud still exist today? What might be its most significant purpose? Even with questions like these, we can hope for vivid messages. One prerequisite for this is that we must not simply allow our intellect to provide the initial answer. In most cases, this would not allow the meaning of the message to be fully grasped. Our insight is often still incomplete at that moment, so it is far more advisable to trust our feelings. This is because the concepts contained in the initial answers are usually symbolic in nature and have corresponding characteristics, but they do not yet answer our questions. Of course, the complexity of our questions will determine the coherence of the overall message. Therefore, the answer will gradually, possibly only after many new experiences, take shape in our mind's eye. The ultimate concrete message that provides the answer to our question may therefore take years to emerge. In any case, this is what our personal experiences have shown us.

By recalling the resurrection of Jesus Christ, the Shroud certainly fulfills an important purpose. We believe it also serves a further purpose.

It is significant that, after so many centuries, the Shroud was first able to be photographed in 1898. That photograph generated fierce controversy and made the Shroud of Turin famous throughout the world. There were doubts about its authenticity because the photographer was suspected of manipulation. It was not until 33 years later that the Shroud was allowed to be photographed again and the unjustified accusations and suspicions could be dispelled. The timing of the first photograph, dating back to the turn of the century, remains interesting. But how can it be understood as a message from the Shroud?

If several causally connected events become evident and comprehensible to us, our emotions will, so to speak, illuminate their significance. If the causal events then also occur within a time frame that we are able to grasp, the emotions that arise give us a feeling about the order of reality. For example, several events that took place in the period around 1900 can be seen to interrelated.

To begin with, for instance, there is the date of origin of the photograph of the Shroud of Turin. Only a short time later, Planck's research triggered the so-called paradigm shift in physics and quantum theory had its birth. In the same year, Nicola Tesla patented his wireless power transmitter. And several future quantum physicists were also born around the same time, all of whom were later honored with the Nobel Prize for their work in quantum physics.

1898 The first photo of the Shroud is taken, a photographic image of Christ

1899 Max Planck discovers the quantum of action

1900 Max Planck establishes quantum theory

1900 Nicola Tesla[19] patents his wireless power transmitter, radio technology is born

1900 Wolfgang Pauli is born; Nobel Prize for the formulation of the Pauli Principle

1901 Werner Heisenberg is born; father of quantum mechanics

1902 Paul Dirac is born; Nobel Prize for the Dirac equation

1903 Marie Curie is awarded a share of the Nobel Prize for Physics

1904 Robert Oppenheimer is born; father of the atomic bomb

1905 Albert Einstein discovers the photoelectric effect

For us, the authors, this opened our eyes to the following message: At the turn of the century, technological progress would enable Christ to reveal Himself on the Shroud worldwide. After almost 2000 years, His face and body would appear, very clearly recognizable, in a "photograph," something that would not have been possible for people to see in this kind of clarity at any earlier time. His appearance also affirms the texts of the Gospels and the New Revelation. Perhaps God appeared at precisely that time because there was an impending threat of earthly chaos. For, at the very beginning of the development of modern physics, that is, at the beginning of the atomic age, God provided a very clear signal with His appearance. And this occurred at a time when science had advanced to the point where the message could be understood. At the very latest, with the evolution of scientific thought regarding energy being equal to matter, the potential of matter to change its state and become energy was to become apparent with the Resurrection. We expect that it is natural at this point that the question will first arise as to why God revealed Himself on the Shroud, but chose not to prevent the looming catastrophes? The findings from Oppenheimer's research, leading to the atomic strikes in Hiroshima and Nagasaki as well as the later nuclear disasters in Chernobyl and Fukushima, prove very emphatically that we humans can indeed act according to our free will.

It is unfortunate for humanity that, following its paradigm shift, science did not become more explicit. The vast amount of knowledge that could be gained, unambiguous and solely related to God, would greatly amplify the content of our general education.

Therefore, for our salvation and well-being, we should demand from our leaders the observance of God's commandments.

Lorber, Mayerhofer and Engel were all Christian heralds of the New Revelation. As Swedenborg achieved with his writings – even in the days before the New Revelation – these mystics proclaimed prophecies to us in the name of and on behalf of God. They revealed the divine order of all living things, the laws governing nature on earth, and the structure and composition of the universe. The extensive explanations contained in the New Revelation were what enabled the author to discern the symbolic emblems on the Shroud of Christ as messages for our time. Her prayers and the loving patience with which she absorbed, in concentrated form, the prophecies of the New Revelation, made it possible for her to spiritually discern the meaning of these symbols on the face of Jesus Christ.

I initially found some of the powerful descriptions in Lorber's revelations unsettling. However, I quickly came to the realization that this demonstrably God-fearing, good man had spent half his life writing down God's words. Why would Lorber deliberately write out thousands of pages of falsehoods? Just the universality in the expression of his depictions made that simply unfathomable. Since then, I have considered it my task to point out the plausibility of the texts of the New Revelation in our book. Lorber and Mayerhofer's writings fill the reader with a sense of harmony and warm-heartedness. Their revelations reveal them to have been true prophets. There is no hint of self-satisfaction in the divine messages and no trace of any interest in worldly fame.

As far as I can judge after only a few months, no significant contradictions can be found among the enormous number of prophecies contained in the New Revelation. On the contrary, my impression is that this spiritual work – like the Shroud of Christ – provides us with messages that help us to understand, in clear terms, the deeper significance of life on earth. We will particularly succeed in this if we are able to accept the meaningful explanations from the Creator that have been given to us as in as calm and objective a manner as possible. The wondrous insights I gained while working on our book have renewed my worldview and expanded my concept of God to a Christian understanding.

In hindsight, the sequence of the entire process can be seen as a necessary progression. Some of the facts and events that I encountered and experienced during the writing process – along with my earlier experiences – were seemingly meant to be included in our book. The interplay between memories from earlier times and my new experiences frequently gave me a feeling of harmony that I find hard to describe. I felt as if my youthful ponderings had finally found their intended destination in the Shroud messages. I often felt as if those earlier mental pictures had been intended for our book from the time of their first appearance. However, it was only during the writing of this final section that I was able to objectively link my memories to the new insights. In the process of deciphering unsolved puzzles and questions, I found myself continually immersed in a seemingly never-ending series of documents and biographies. I pored through reports and books for information from and about prominent scientists. In the beginning, I was interested in concepts related to "matter." I wanted to understand how scientists comprehend and explain the structure of matter, because it had ultimately become clear to me that matter actually does not exist.

Later, I became much more interested in the personal beliefs and worldviews of these scientists. This arose out of my fascination with certain parts of the prophetic insights found in the New Revelation. These fit in perfectly with my worldview and my understanding of our Creator. All of the revelations given us through Lorber and Mayerhofer have something in common: the style and character of the writing as well as the impressions gained from the explanations are always reasonable and plausible. This is especially evident in the description of the ingenious plan for Creation and the guidelines revealed for the divine order. The extraordinary simplicity of this order is ingenious. With each new chapter of the New Revelation that I absorbed myself in, my imagination took wings. My intuition told me that among the clever minds of the scientific community there must surely be some who would say they agree with God's theses and, that they agree in particular because His messages clearly reflect our experiences of reality.

So far, there has not yet been a scientific explanation for the question of why it is that matter does not actually exist, but still can be perceived by us. It may be important to note that the most minute elements involved in holding the earth together at its core are still not detectable at the subatomic level. Even after more than a century of research, researchers have not been able to accomplish this. That which has been able to be shown in this regard is the culmination of the various assumptions they have been able to make on the basis of their work. Scientists conclude that the elementary particles responsible for the bonding together and formation of what we are able to perceive are not matter. Allegedly, the composition of these elements can be mathematically and measurably recorded as an energy field. And the forces active within the field are said to produce what we perceive with our senses as physical matter. The particle physicists of our day refer to the crucial, but in actuality, not verifiably massless, energy particles as gluons, also known as atomic "glue". Researchers have been unable to detect unattached individual gluons, making it very difficult to empirically prove the existence of these particles.

It is equally obvious that it is impossible to accept (or want to accept) what might also be the case here. It is difficult to avoid the impression that some scientists consider it their task to produce evidence that would exclude the presence of a divine Creator.

Awakening Awareness

At first, I was completely fascinated by the significant findings in the fields of quantum physics and relativity theory. However, presenting the detailed research results from modern physics was beyond the scope of this book. It would be impossible for us, as non-physicists, to provide any useful explanations. Even today, physicists are still trying to explain why matter, as materialists understand it, actually does not exist. In their quantum theory experiments, scientists use probability values for their calculations. The results cannot be predicted more precisely, because they only become apparent during the course of the experiment. It should nevertheless be borne in mind that results from these complex experiments are obtained using axiomatic derivatives of mathematical equations.

From Werner Heisenberg's writings, I learned that mathematical results should actually be regarded as analytical assessments that cannot represent reality. We should also remember that today, computer software is commonly used in virtually all scientific studies, and many process steps are reduced to complex, mathematical formulas. These abstract computational methods make it impossible to explain, in generally understandable language, events in the micro- and macrocosm, especially the origin of matter. Evidently, individual components of reality can be made visible, but not the whole picture. We must always keep in mind that everything around us, now and in the future, is in a constant state of creative development. This also applies, of course, to terms used in the languages of all cultural communities.

To be able to consciously perceive moving events, we need a sufficient amount of time. To measure earthly duration, we humans use a system that we have devised ourselves, which we refer to as "time." To find suitable terms for new insights or even to be able to develop them, also takes time. If this were not the case, we would never be able to talk about new ideas. The overriding principle of causality, through which we see every effect as having an explainable cause, had to be discarded because of ambiguous findings from atomic experiments. Is this perhaps just for now, or merely an exception? To a certain extent, the Big Bang hypothesis is also based on this principle. As I understand it, the concept of "privilege" – a possible effect without any plausible cause – has actually led to an in-

teresting concession from the scientific community: if observed atten-
tively, such abstract methods can be used to present the facts about advanced assessments of reality in an equally simple manner. But if they
are only formulated similarly to the Big Bang theory, when it comes to
God, researchers would consider us to have exceeded the limits of our
experiences and consciousness.

A revelation given to Mayerhofer during a sermon:

> That My listeners then were not very fertile soil for My teaching I was quite
> aware of; but I knew that I was not speaking and acting only for them, but for
> all mankind after them. I did not build for that time alone; My plans were
> reaching much farther. As the plans of a divine, infinite Being, they were ever-
> lasting and eternally effective.
>
> To their request for a miraculous sign, I even answered to the Pharisees and
> scribes that this generation would not be given a sign by Me, which meant
> that where My visible appearance was the greatest miraculous sign, no addi-
> tional proof of My deity and the truth and everlasting continuance of My tea-
> ching was needed.
>
> And what I then told the Pharisees and scribes, applies also today to all hypo-
> critical churchgoers and to all the scholars of your time developing their phi-
> losophies about matter. They, too, will not be seeing any signs because they do
> not want to accept the greatest sign, the voice of a God and Father in their
> own hearts. Thus, many of your scientists, notwithstanding the constant dis-
> coveries of laws of nature, do not believe that there must also be a lawgiver.
> They would rather dispute their own self away than admit defeat through
> factual evidence of the existence of God.[20]

---

1   Synchronicity is the term used when two or more events occur simultaneously and
    there is no external, causal relationship (cause-and-effect relationship), but rather, an
    inner connection. According to C.G. Jung, synchronicities are not to be explained in
    terms of luck or coincidence but should be understood as messages that we are meant
    to put to use.

2   Planck, Max: *Vortraege und Erinnerungen, Religion und Naturwissenschaft, IV*, p. 331,
    translation by C. Dyre

3   Translator's note: In Germany, the state-sponsored churches are supported through
    the German Church Tax.

4   Translator's note: In some of Germany's federal states, Religion is taught as a part of
    the public school curriculum.

5   Kupsch, F. R.: *Lehrbuch und Atlas Der Anatomie. Nervensysteme – Sinnesorgane.* Volume III. Figure 88, p. 77 and Figure 128, p. 124.

6   Ibid.

7   Taken from Hermann, Joachim: *Astronomie die uns angeht,* p. 270

8   See Endnote 5.

9   https://en.wikipedia.org/wiki/Antennae_Galaxies (accessed Nov. 12, 2020)

10 https://de.wikipedia.org/wiki/Centaurus_A;   http://www.eso.org/public/outreach/press-rel/copyright.html. By ESO/WFI (Optical); MPIfR/ESO/APEX/ A.Weiss et al. (accessed Nov. 12, 2020).

11 Mayerhofer, Gottfried, *Secrets of Life, p.* 140, translator unknown. EPUB book downloaded from https://archive.org/details/6.ebooksecretsoflife (accessed Nov. 12, 2020).

12 Einstein, Albert, *The Human Side,* p. 33.

13 Lorber, *Himmelsgaben,* 3, 640408, 24, translation by the author.

14 Mayerhofer, Gottfried, *Secrets of Life, p.* 38, translator unknown. EPUB book downloaded from https://archive.org/details/6.ebooksecretsoflife (accessed Nov. 12, 2020).

15 http://www.weloennig.de/MaxPlanck.html#3 (accessed Nov. 1, 2019) The source cited on the website given is the *Archiv zur Geschichte der Max-Planck-Gesellschaft, Abt. Va, Rep. 11 Planck, Nr. 1797.* An audio recording of the lecture can be found on YouTube (in German): *Max Planck: "... denn die Materie bestuende ohne den Geist ueberhaupt nicht."* Published on March 20, 2014. (accessed August 3, 2019.)

16 Einstein, Albert, *The World As I See* It, Alan Harris (Transl.) https://play.google.com/store/books/details?id=Y_9kDwAAQBAJ&rdid=book-Y_9kDwAAQBAJ&rdot=1&source=gbs_vpt_read&pcampaignid=books_booksearch_viewport (accessed Nov. 12, 2020).

17 Einstein, Albert, in *Science, Philosophy and Religion: A Symposium. The Conference on Science, Philosophy and Religion in Their Relation to the Democratic Way of Life, Inc.,* New York, 1941. https://www.update.uu.se/~fbendz/lib rary/ae_ scire.htm (accessed Nov. 12, 2020).

18 St. Apollinare in Classe. https://commons.wikimedia.org/wiki/File:Ravenna_BW_3.JPG. Public domain, by Berthold Werner – own work. (accessed Nov. 12, 2020)

19 **Beginning in 1875, Nikola Tesla (1856–1943) studied for about three years at the Technical University in Graz, Austria.** Whether it was there that he came into contact with the works of Jakob Lorber is not known to us. It is interesting to note that Tesla had a completely new conception of energy types. His secret understanding of the forces of nature can unfortunately not be explained. In any case, it enabled him to develop countless inventions that still have a great impact on our technological world today. *"The day when science begins to study non-physical phenomena, it will make more progress in a decade than in any previous century of its existence. **In order to understand the true nature of the universe, it must be considered as energy, frequency and vibration.**"* Nikola Tesla

20 Mayerhofer, *The Lord's Sermons,* translation by the author.

Scientific Affirmations of the New Revelation

My youthful worldview, in which the force responsible for the Creation emanated from a galactic consciousness, was admittedly illusory. And yet, this fanciful concept can be interwoven with various threads of revelations that have been made by quantum theorists as well as those in the New Revelation.

In the New Revelation, God's words explain earthly and human values to us through consistently worthy interpretations of their meaning. In addition, they contain practical wisdom to provide us with guidance and lead us on our path through life. One of the most brilliant and special aspects of this is that, in the form of reasonable commandments, all of this is given us to allow us to freely make our own decisions. This aspect, when consistently thought out, combined with the free will we have been granted, allows us to recognize the successful and secure planning of our Creator.

The love of neighbor and the love of God, combined with the free will that has been given to humanity, represent the most effective foundation for a successful life. The honoring and acceptance of these simple commandments provides the most significant assurance for achieving the Divine goals and the stability they provide.

The Commandment of Love

In keeping with this, below is an excerpt from Mayerhofer's book *The Lord's Sermons*. God's greatest and most noble commandment consists of the two commandments to love.

For the 17th Sunday of the Trinity, April 24, 1872, Mayerhofer revealed the underlying principles and the actual meaning of these two commandments to love. (Note: I had been familiar with the commandment to love your neighbor as yourself since my childhood. However, I never really understood the implications of this commandment – to love others as yourself – to our success in life! One simple explanation for this may be that you can only ever give others what you yourself possess! This is also something I had not adequately considered before. However, it seems to me that this explanation alone is hardly sufficient to allow us to fully understand everything.)

In this sermon, the Lord confides to Mayerhofer that these two commandments are not easy to understand. We therefore need to first ask: "Why are we meant to love God above all else?" Just the compelling openness of this confident declaration alone, as contained in these revelatory writings, illustrates the sacred character of the Divine soul.

> Considering the question: "Why should I love God?" – the coldly reasoning person will answer: "Thinking about it, I actually find no reason why I should love God. Firstly, because I cannot love something invisible and, secondly, I do not owe any gratitude to the God Who created me, for He did not ask whether it suited me or not. He had only His pleasure of creating in mind and did not ask whether I, as the created being, would really be satisfied with My condition and the position He assigned to me among the other created beings, and whether I am feeling happy."
> From these conclusions it would follow that there would be no obligation for man to love his Creator, even if He had placed him in the most fortunate circumstances, and much less so considering the hardships, suffering and misfortunes man has to struggle with from birth to death. Should men love God for that, and even "above everything"? That would be asking too much! There are people who would like to say to their Creator: "If you had not created me as a human being you might still claim my love, but in these sad living conditions it would require just too much simplicity to love Him Who in some respects placed me below the animal, yet gave me the ability to be really conscious of my state and to deplore it!"
> Behold, My children, this is the not unjustified opinion of the rationalist whose world is the cold reality, that is, what he sees before him, can touch with his hands and perceive with his senses.[1]

Mayerhofer explains that, ever since the first human beings were created, this type of thinking had always been the basis for individual behavior. In the following, he reveals, in God-given words, that the greatest and most groundbreaking of God's laws acts to serve love, the perpetuation of Creation, cohesion, and perfection!

> Now, if I as the Creator lay down love as the principle law for My created beings that are like Me, love for their Creator, it is obvious that the reason for this law must also be recognizable in My instructions and a person must understand that – whatever happens – love is at the root of everything.
> What actually is "love"? We have to clarify also this concept to give us a better judgment concerning it.

Love is nothing else but a certain attachment to an animate or inanimate object. This attachment safeguards the preservation of this object to that degree to which it lays claim to our love. Among living beings love is an attachment or attraction to other beings with whom, due to their nature, there is emotional harmony. In the case of humans, the one who gives love also receives it in return. The loving person wants to remain with the loved one in a state of interchange with his thinking and feeling and, receiving love in return, as it were, unite with that person to form a spiritual whole. Love which has no other goal than to see the loved one as happy as possible is also the quality that enables us to give the loved one everything, retaining nothing but the conviction of having made that person as happy as we can.

Only when a person has comprehended this love on the part of his God, Creator and Lord, can he easily understand the law of love demanding of him to love with all his heart and with the greatest possible intensity the God Who has given everything to make His created beings happy for all eternity.

But how does God prove this love which He has sacrificed for man to stimulate his human love into loving the Creator of the great universe above everything, above all that is of the world, the visible and invisible.[2]

He goes on to explain the ways in which God demonstrates his love for us and how, in becoming Jesus Christ, he evidenced this. Two possible pathways are shown us. These lead through both the spiritual, invisible world that dwells within us and the material, visible world that surrounds us. Although different in expression, both paths lead to the same goal: to understand the Creator as our loving Lord and Father.

Let us now examine the first way.

In former times, when man's knowledge of nature was still more limited, scientists discovered many a starting point for the infinite, on a large scale as well as on a small scale. In those times it was the inner man with whom the enthusiastic lawgivers, like Moses, the Prophets and the seers, concerned themselves. They drew man's attention to his inner life and established as a law what men should actually do of their own accord.

In those times, this commandment of love for God was presented to men as a law, not as a commandment of love. That is why the Pharisee asked which was the greatest commandment, since he did not consider this one so important and may have believed he might receive an answer from Me referring to some civil law. For love, as I demanded it, was unknown to this Pharisee and to many other people in those times. Thus, notwithstanding these enlightened times, to millions of the people living today love, which means something different from self-love, is an unknown thing.

In order to make this law of My great creation known and recognized, I Myself descended to your dark earth and demonstrated through word and deed what love for God and love for one's fellowman actually means. Thus I turned man away from his materialistic tendency and raised him to a spiritual being with its roots, its feet, on earth in the material, but lifting its head, or the spiritual flower, into regions that have no connection with matter.

Just as I explained the love of God to My contemporaries, I showed them through numerous parables, words and deeds what the love of one's neighbor is and how it must be understood and practiced. I showed them how the second commandment of love for one's neighbor can only be fulfilled if first the love of God has been fully conceived in its spiritual meaning and how, vice versa, the love of God can only be genuine and pure if it is expressed as brotherly love for one's fellowmen and all the surrounding world.

The second way to prove God's love through nature, recognizing in it His voice on every step, was reserved for later centuries, although already at the time of My life on earth, and earlier still, the priesthood was more familiar with the secrets of nature than many people are even today. This voice, through which I wanted to give men countless proofs of My all-embracing love, remained unnoticed for a long time. Even now only few hear this voice in their explorations. **Unfortunately, most of those who rake about in the field of natural science know only matter and the laws imposed upon it by Me, instead of hearing the soft call of love breathing to them from every atom,** since a breath of love from My divine Self is latent in every atom, awaiting its further development in accordance with the laws of love.

It was the telescope which opened up the vast expanses above for you who are living today; and it was the microscope which revealed to you the wonders of the minutest things. With the help of both instruments you may be able to guess, but not comprehend, infinity and the Infinite Himself. Both sciences – astronomy and natural science – have been given to man to dampen his pride, to eliminate his self-conceit and still raise him high above all spaces as a spirit, since they enabled the finite to guess and conceive the infinite.

Both sciences are meant to lead to the love of God, the love of God to human dignity and human dignity to the love of one's neighbor, which again leads back to Him Who has arranged everything in such a way that every spark of love can complete its circuit by returning to Me as God from Whom it has originated. Thus the love of God is to form spontaneously in the hearts of men and express itself in the love of one's neighbor which – based on the former – speeds up the circuit, and in this way both laws, out of which everything has originated and to which everything seeks to return, prove to be truly the supreme and sole laws. Consequently, they are the noblest laws since they are based on love, on the inclination of like toward like and, therefore, can only give harmony, that is, peace, bliss and delight.

Even if man in the course of his life has to put up with many a struggle and

bitter suffering, the spiritually inclined person does not regard this as the result of material or social circumstances, but sees in it an education for a higher life. The temptations of the material world must first be overcome before
it is possible to comprehend the spiritual world in all its significance. Thus for
him, the son of a God, struggles and suffering are only a spur to progress, not
a cause for disappointment; thus he feels sublime in the struggles with a material world and, as a spiritual child of an eternally loving Father, strong
enough to conquer them, for the corroboration of which I, as Jesus, have given you a splendid example.

In this state of awareness man understands why he should love God above all,
that is, far above every other love; why he should regard the love of God as the
highest and comply with its demands. He also understands why he should
love his neighbor who, too, is a spiritual being, gone forth from the hand of
God like himself, which means, he should respect him just as he himself, as
the image of God, wishes to be regarded and respected.

Thus you shall love Me as God and prove this love on your neighbor so that
you may be true descendants of Him Who has breathed His wonders into all
things. Then you will realize that a world can only exist if its basic nature is
love, if love is its impulse for existence and perfection.

It is this which My two commandments preach to you, what they are telling
you in a thousand ways from the cradle to the grave and what they will be rei-
terating far beyond this life – that without love there cannot be a Father nor
can there be children. Amen.

Even before I finished reading this chapter in the New Revelation, it became clear to me that the commandment to love must indeed be called the
greatest of all God's commandments. Just as Mayerhofer tells us, our scientific knowledge should lead us first to the love of God, from the love of God
to human dignity, and from human dignity to the love of our neighbor.
Some individual scientists have attempted this. If we look at the second
path described in this sermon, this is what I believe Heisenberg recognized
so well. The cosmic order, as he calls it, has, if we take its individual parts as
a whole, a character within which all events taking place in the universe
can, independently and by means of simple rules, always realign themselves in a positive direction (please also see Endnote 42 on p. 192).

Just think what people can achieve through altruism alone. Last but
not least, this thought makes it clear that we have an indispensable and
ideal solution for safeguarding communal life. As Mayerhofer's revelation shows, without love, neither human life nor earthly life would be
possible, and no further progress could take place.

I believe that wholehearted acceptance of this commandment is the best possible means for us to successfully coexist. Taking a broad view, all of the other commandments, those that tell us what we should do or what we should not do, would be best fulfilled by simply loving our neighbor as ourselves. This human bond is what will make it possible for us to enduringly and successfully coexist.

In addition, the free will God has given us allows us, through our own independent decisions, without fear, to come to know this internally harmonized order, so that we might happily live under the simplest of all possible rules and with a desire to love our neighbor!

The epilogue to the 53 sermons in *The Lord's Sermons* confirmed what I was thinking:

> The words put down here will always give you peace and comfort, although, perhaps, not instantly. They will often give you the incentive and serve as a guide to how peace can be gained. These sermons are meant to be like steps which by and by will teach you to know Me, My Words and yourselves ever better and enhance your insight; for eons of time would not suffice to explain all that is contained in My sole two commandments of love.[3]

In Kurt Eggenstein's book, *The Unknown Prophet Jakob Lorber*, I learned that some of his other scientific revelations have also been proven true and confirmed by scientists. The author summarizes the mystical messages of the New Revelation in a most interesting way. In contrast, however, scientific descriptions that go beyond this have not been able to show me, in a way I can understand, what, from the perspective of research, actually constitutes reality. Several hypotheses have been proven to be erroneous and have had to be retracted. However, I did not want to let this fact bring a halt to my search. My attempts to compare hard-to-follow scientific texts with the New Revelation meant that this phase took much longer than I had previously estimated. I wanted to emphasize the special significance of the New Revelation, because the scientific prophecies, including those regarding matter, had already been documented in writing by Jakob Lorber decades before their discovery by the scientific community. I wanted to be able to prove through these comparisons that, in addition to Lorber and Mayerhofer's scientific predictions, their spiritual religious revelations could also be accepted as divine messages.

After months of struggling with these comparisons, I finally realized that no matter how many more affirmations I could find in the research, they would still not achieve what we wanted to show through our writings on the Shroud messages. For us, the abundance of evidence proves beyond a doubt the authenticity of the Shroud. I therefore decided I would simply examine the personal, private views and religious-philosophical worldviews of a number of prominent scientists. I was no longer interested in objective understanding. Just as in my youth, I wanted to primarily rely on consciously experienced feelings.

In the context of scientific findings, Werner Heisenberg's philosophies, for example, his "uncertainty relation," in combination with Goethe's "order of reality," can provide us with a solid picture of his religious worldview. In our opinion, this is an important piece of information that still receives far too little attention. Basically, Gisela and I now regard scientists like Planck, Einstein, and Heisenberg to be modern-day mystics. In the following sections, I will attempt to convey this intuitive impression to the reader, using Heisenberg as an example. With every chapter I read regarding the achievements and pronouncements of this brilliant researcher, my impressions were reinforced. It was as though a visionary had suddenly explained to us the unique characteristics of reality.

Additional quotations have been selected to demonstrate how scientific findings can be reconciled with the concepts expressed in the New Revelation. At this point, it must be noted that the individual pieces of our collected findings naturally cannot reveal exactly things that could only be made clear by looking at the respective literature as a whole. However, key individual clues, when viewed in combination, can help to open many a difficult door to the New Revelation. The various quotations from the New Revelation as well as those from the scientists' writings are meant to demonstrate that reality can be ordered not only with the human mind, but even more so with our conscious feelings.

Max Planck

This excerpt from one of Planck's lectures reveals how this great physicist saw the world:

In summary, we can state that physical science demands the assumption of a real world, independent of us, which we can never directly discern, but can always only perceive through the lens of our sensory perceptions and the measurements they convey.

If we pursue this statement further, the manner in which we observe the world takes on a different form. The subject of observation, the observing ego, moves away from the center of thought and is relegated to a very modest place.

Indeed, how pitifully small, how powerless we human beings must seem to ourselves when we consider that the earth upon which we live constitutes only a minuscule speck of dust, almost nothing, in the utterly immeasurable universe, and how strange it must seem to us, on the other hand, that we, tiny creatures on a random tiny planet, are able to discern with our thoughts not the essence, but the presence and size of the elementary building blocks of the entire vast world.[4]

Mayerhofer tells us that the Lord said to His disciples:

Be prepared, My children, wherever you may be – here on earth or in the beyond – to celebrate with Me this feast of resurrection of the spiritual dignity of man. For it is not only the greatest feast for mankind, but also the most important for My entire great spirit-kingdom, when this final act will prove why I once descended to your small earth and why I chose you, unprepossessing and tiny beings on a grain of sand orbiting in infinite space, to become My children.[5]

Planck continues:

But the miracle is even greater. Research in physical science has proven beyond any doubt that these elementary building blocks of the cosmic edifice are not arranged side by side in individual groups with no connection, but that they are all connected in accordance with a single plan, or in other words, that in all natural processes, a universal law prevails, which we, to a certain degree, are able to discern.[6]

Mayerhofer:

As I once performed the greatest act of love in My creation with you poor, little mites, so also you shall endeavor in the smallest things, even insignificant events, to follow My commandments of love and carry them out promptly and conscientiously, so that you, too, may show and prove in the smallest the great strength of your souls. Then you are My worthy children, who one day can be set over great things, where you can then spread peace and bliss on a large scale, since you did that on your small earth under humble conditions.[7]

Planck's lecture, from which the excerpts above are taken, touched me very much. It was in this lecture that I first learned about the phenomenon of modern physics. And, the religious passion of his speeches was no less impressive to me. In any case, this speech was the impetus for my continued research. I was able to draw from the revelations of Lorber and Mayerhofer just as vividly as I was with Planck's writings. Kurt Eggenstein's book is, in my opinion, the optimal source for gaining a solid overview of the revelations and their corroboration.[8]

As I have already said, I hoped that the substance of what was at that time a phenomenal novelty might also have inspired other researchers to make public observations similar to those of Max Planck. I believed that the writings of brilliant physicists would not reveal any conclusions that would contradict Planck's. In fact, I was not entirely wrong in this regard.

1 Mayerhofer, Gottfried, *The Lord's Sermons*, pp. 269-276, translation by the author

2 Ibid.

3   Ibid., p. 335 [Eons are defined as the longest period of time]

4 Planck, Max, *Vortrage und Erinnerungen*, p. 327, translation by C. Dyre

5 Mayerhofer, Gottfried, *The Lord's Sermons*, p. 171, translation by the author

6 Planck, Max. *Vortrage und Erinnerungen*, p. 327, translation by C. Dyre

7 Mayerhofer, Gottfried:, *The Lord's Sermons*, pp. 269-276, translation by the author

8 Eggenstein, Kurt and Ozols, Violet, *The Unknown Prophet Jakob Lorber*. Merkur Publishing Inc., Salt Lake City. 1979.

Where Relativity, Quantum Theory and Christian Mysticism Intersect

In the following chapter, I would like to compare statements made by three renowned physicists with the theses presented in Lorber and Mayerhofer's New Revelation. In particular, one of the physicists, Werner Heisenberg, moved me most in this regard.

Hans Peter Duerr

The books and Internet films by and featuring Hans Peter Duerr are both remarkable and impressive. This physics professor (October 7, 1929 – May 18, 2014) was a student of Werner Heisenberg and was also a recipient of the Alternative Nobel Prize. He worked for many years alongside Werner Heisenberg, during Professor Heisenberg's tenure as director of the Max Planck Institute in Munich, later succeeding him in this position. Duerr obviously gained his cumulative knowledge of quantum theory while working as a member of Heisenberg's team. My understanding of Duerr is that he also adopted the majority of Heisenberg's philosophical ideas. In his publications, I often recognize Heisenberg's voice.

His published personal and philosophical findings are particularly interesting. The YouTube video "Matter does not exist"[1] is especially informative, as are many of the other of his videos in the German language, such as "Es gibt nichts Unschoepferisches" ("Nothing Is Inexhaustible") and "Ueber das Lebendige, den geronnenen Geist und die ordnende Hand" ("Concerning the living, the coagulated spirit, and the organizing hand").

We had submitted our manuscript to the editor for an initial review. I procured for myself a large stack of books, which I intended to use as references for information about the scientists whose statements were featured in Duerr's book. I soon realized, however, that this information went beyond the intended scope of our book. Nevertheless, as I read through some of these books, it became clear to me that many researchers, including some who had been Nobel laureates, had, in the course of their work, discovered God to be the Creator of the world. I had already read several books by and about Planck, and a number of quotations from his writings indicated what the fruits of his life's work meant for him. While I was searching through the quotations, it soon became evident that Planck was categorically convinced that the force holding our world together at its core is a God-given energy.

Duerr's anthology *Physik und Transzendenz* ("Physics and Transcendence") is a compilation of essays from authors who all belonged to the same cultural sphere. Even more so, according to Duerr: "They are all physicists whose life's work was closely linked to the paradigm shift from classical physics to quantum physics or at least was strongly influenced by it."[2] This anthology also illustrates the enthusiasm and affection Duerr held for Heisenberg. Quite deliberately, Heisenberg's essays do not appear until the final section of the book. Two of these essays were taken from his biography. However, in the final chapter, the anthology's ultimate conclusion consists of a philosophical manuscript by Heisenberg, which he finished writing in the fall of 1942, but never published himself.

So that we could complete our work as quickly as possible, after finishing my study of Planck, I focused solely on comparing Einstein's thoughts and Heisenberg's writings to the New Revelation.

Albert Einstein

I next read *The Universe and Dr. Einstein*, by Lincoln Barnett. Einstein's mindset and his worldview, as described in the book, were a special discovery for me. One of his quotations in particular illustrates Einstein's characteristic outlook. As long as he lived, he remained unconvinced by the mathematical calculations that, in quantum theory, provide probability results for the atom, and he justified this with his famous saying: "The Old One does not play dice." When he spoke of God in German, he referred to God as "the Old One," as he did here.

Einstein's personal worldview is impressive in this respect. Barnett summarizes it in chapter XV:[3]

> Cosmologists for the most part maintain silence on the question of ultimate origins, leaving that issue to the philosophers and theology. Yet only the purest empiricists among modern scientists turn their backs on the mystery that

underlies physical reality. Einstein, whose philosophy of science has some- times been criticized as materialistic, once said:

"The most beautiful and most profound emotion we can experience is the
sensation of the mystical. It is the sower of all true science. He to whom this
emotion is a stranger, who can no longer wonder and stand rapt in awe, is as
good as dead. To know that what is impenetrable to us really exists, manifes-
ting itself as the highest wisdom and the most radiant beauty which our dull
faculties can comprehend only in their most primitive forms – this
knowledge, this feeling is at the centre of true religiousness."

And on another occasion, Barnett writes:

"The cosmic religious experience is the strongest and noblest mainspring of
scientific research."[4]

The majority of physicists tend to avoid the word God when discussing
the mysteries of the universe, its tremendous forces, its origin, its rational structure, and its harmony. Einstein, however, who has been
dubbed an atheist, has no such inhibitions. He says:

My religion [...] consists of **a humble admiration of the illimitable superior
spirit** who reveals Himself in the slight details we are able to perceive with
our frail and feeble minds. That deeply emotional conviction of the presence
of a superior reasoning power, which is revealed in the incomprehensible
universe, forms my idea of God.[5]

How are we to assess Einstein's position on and attitude toward the question of religion and faith? In Barnett's writings, it becomes clear that
Einstein considered himself a religious person, albeit according to his
own definition of religion. We can find this religious mindset and similar ideological opinions in a number of books written by and about him.

Einstein rejected the idea of a personal God. As he often said, his religion was characterized by awe and humble amazement at the harmony
of nature, not by belief in a personal God who dictates the lives of individuals.

It is very difficult to explain this feeling [his cosmic religious feeling] to
anyone who is entirely without it...[6]

Einstein's view on faith or religion is best described in one of his statements, in which he referred to himself as "agnostic."[7] Agnostic, in the
sense that he did not believe in the existence of a personal God. However,

he also doubted in the free will of humans. Einstein was convinced that in nature, there is a prevailing order rooted in natural laws. It continually amazed him; for him, everything, without exception, was governed by causal connections (cause and effect).

Much of what he said signaled that his worldview was always characterized by a religious sense of humanity. In *The World As I See It*, Einstein reveals that he reveres the teachings of Jesus Christ: "If one purges the Judaism of the Prophets and Christianity as Jesus Christ taught it of all subsequent additions, especially those of the priests, one is left with a teaching which is capable of curing all the social ills of humanity." He called this "the teaching of pure humanity."[8]

Like Heisenberg, Einstein also acknowledged:

> "The more a man is imbued with the ordered regularity of all events the firmer becomes his conviction that there is no room left by the side of this ordered regularity for causes of a different nature."[9]

Werner Heisenberg's Perspective on the Creation

I got far more out of Heisenberg's biography than I had ever anticipated.

Physics and Beyond

I find Heisenberg's formulations of his ideas and his writing style to be brilliant. I should mention up front that his explanations of religion remained a more scientific depiction until the end of his chronicle *Physics and Beyond*. In his writings on religious matters in this book, he resolutely avoids mentioning any Creator God. On questions regarding the existence of a personal God, he responded with a description of a soul, which was perceptible to him in the unquestionable cosmic order. Nevertheless, in some passages of the text, I detected a profound, religious line of thought. Similar to Einstein, Heisenberg, when discussing natural laws, describes a singular simplicity of the cosmic order of things and events in nature. He describes a special clarity that can be discerned from the laws of nature:

> However, I do not know if I can express myself correctly and understandably here. If, as is always the case in theoretical physics, you summarize the results

of experiments in formulas and thus arrive at a phenomenological description of the processes, you have the impression that you have invented these formulas yourself, with more or less gratifying success. But when one encounters these very simple large correlations, which are ultimately fixed in axiomatic theory, things look quite different. In our mind's eye, **a connection suddenly appears, which had always been there, even without us, and which is obviously not of human origin.** Such connections are surely the true substance of our science. Only when one has fully absorbed the existence of such connections can one really understand our science.[10]

In other places in the book, as in his discussions with Wolfgang Pauli, he indicates that his concepts had their roots in the language of ancient religions. They are to be viewed as images and metaphors, not as scientific explanations. He frequently remarked that he did not want to be misunderstood if he were to use words such as "plan or soul" when discussing the incontestable cosmic order.

In my opinion, throughout the book, but especially in the middle section, Heisenberg presents some core ideas, which he perhaps consciously intended would illuminate readers and be passed on to future scientists. In the chapter "Positivism, Metaphysics, and Religion," he writes about a conference that was held in Copenhagen in the spring of 1952. While in attendance, he often took long walks with Wolfgang Pauli, during which they held discussions about philosophy or quantum theory. In one paragraph, I felt that Heisenberg was almost addressing me personally. During a break in a conversation with his friend Wolfgang on the philosophy of positivism, he posed various witty questions to himself in a kind of soliloquy. I found the following line of thought particularly interesting:

> Is it completely pointless **to conceive by and large of a "consciousness"** behind the organizing structures of the world, **whose "intention" they are**?[11]

Even after reading this line several times, I was still quite astonished and very pleased. In his biography, this prominent scientist had questioned that which was at the very core of my youthful worldview! At no other place in this book does it seem to me to be more appropriate to cite the following passage from the New Revelation. For the Ninth Sunday of the Trinity:

> The keenest over-subtle reasoners, natural scientists, and explorers of matter, despite their resistance, all do and must come to realize in the end that high

above matter there dwells a great spirit who unites the smallest atoms as well as the great worlds to a whole and who, as can be seen from all his works, can only be a God of love, grace and forbearance and – as was once stated in the parable of the prodigal son He rejoices more over one regained than over ninety-nine righteous, who do not need to be comforted. "THERE IS A GOD!" This call resounds from everything.[12]

Actually, in Heisenberg's writings on consciousness, he only ever described his hypothetical thoughts. No more, but certainly no less! I do not thereby impute to Heisenberg any concept of a divine Creator. Not yet. He goes on to explain in the same line:

Of course, posed in this manner, the question is also a humanization of the problem, because the word "consciousness" is, after all, formed from human experience. Consequently, this term should not be used outside the human realm. But, if one were to be so restrictive, it would also become impermissible to speak, for example, of the consciousness of an animal. Nevertheless, there is a feeling that such a way of speaking does make a certain amount of sense. It is felt that the meaning of the term "consciousness" is thereby expanded while, at the same time, it becomes hazier when we try to apply it outside of the human realm. For positivists, then, there is a simple solution: the world must be divided into that which can be unequivocally stated and that about which we must remain silent. Thus, here, one would simply have to remain silent. However, there is possibly no philosophy more absurd than this one. *Because almost nothing can be stated unequivocally. When all ambiguity has been eliminated, the only thing that is likely to remain are utterly uninteresting tautologies.*[13]

In their discussions, Pauli raised further questions about the religious values and the factual basis that shaped Heisenberg's concept of truth. Among other things, Pauli questioned the justifications for Heisenberg's theses. Suddenly, rather abruptly, Pauli asked his friend: "Do you actually believe in a personal God?"

Heisenberg replied: "May I phrase the question differently? Then, I would ask: Can you, or can anyone. counter the essential order of things or events, which is beyond dispute, as directly as is possible with the soul of another human being? I am explicitly using the word soul here, which is so difficult to interpret, to avoid being misunderstood. If you put it that way, I would answer "yes."[14]

Reality and Its Order

After reading Heisenberg's professional memoirs, I thought I understood: He was obviously a scientist who had been influenced by Christianity. With great anticipation, I now sought to learn more about him, and so I purchased his book *Reality and Its Order*. However, in contrast to his professional biography, in this book, Heisenberg, in my opinion, gives the impression that he was acquainted with texts of the New Revelation.

Now, before I get ahead of myself, I would like to draw attention to the initial sections of the book. There, the editors explain that ever since his youth, Heisenberg had been greatly impressed by the writings of the great German poet, Goethe, and that the entire system behind *Reality and Its Order* had been adopted from Goethe. Goethe, in turn, had already been studying the writings of the mystic Emanuel Swedenborg by the time he was twenty. Over the course of more than fifty years, Goethe adapted many of Swedenborg's ideas into his life's work, most notably in his tragedy, "Faust."

Reality and Its Order is the first of a total of five volumes. These *Philosophical and Popular Writings* – about half of the texts were being published in book form for the first time – were primarily intended for laypersons with an interest in the natural sciences. They contain fascinating insights into the thinking of this Nobel laureate. In addition to speeches and essays on the fundamentals and interpretation of physics, the works reveal his overall view of the concept of nature as it has developed from ancient times to the present.

To begin with, it can be said that in these writings the atmosphere of suspense Heisenberg achieves at the beginning of the book never diminishes on a single page. It is uncertain whether Heisenberg would have selected this particular title for his book –it was chosen by the editors. In any case, it is clear that in this essay he was obviously preoccupied by questions surrounding the problem of how the whole, which we would call the world or life, is interconnected, and where within this whole, the particular connections are to be found.

As he does in his essays and lectures, Heisenberg frequently takes a stand on questions that go beyond the scope and narrow boundaries of his scientific discipline. And not least, his use of the language, as one of the 20th century's most prominent scientists, the father of quantum mechanics and a Nobel Prize laureate in Physics, reveals a distinctive view of the world. This view, as wide-ranging as it is profound, seemingly requires the intellectual capacity of a brilliant mathematician, combined with a great musical talent. I found some of Heisenberg's statements in his essay *Reality and Its Order* particularly instructive. Here, both his philosophical thinking and the structuring of his worldview are almost perfectly organized and summarized into sections.

Unfortunately, it is nearly impossible to quote from such a wide-ranging, vivid philosophy in such a way that it does not at some point move beyond its actual context. However, with the quotations we have chosen, it is our sincere intention to demonstrate how some scientific findings can be compared – and sometimes even conform – with the prophecies of the New Revelation. This becomes especially apparent in Heisenberg's conclusions, which he draws from a number of domains of reality, as well as in his recognition of the creative forces we humans possess.

Heisenberg and Goethe

Heisenberg's wife, Elisabeth, explains in her remarks on the content of the book that "Goethe accompanied him throughout his life."[15] In the same chapter, Rechenberg, the editor, explains:

> **It should be noted, of course, that Heisenberg adopted from Goethe the whole system of the "order of reality."** One reason for this may be his predilection for the poet's works, another may be his basic conviction:

> "It is probably more accurate to assume that all truly great natural scientists were quite familiar with the language of poetry as well. Thus, the poet [Goethe] provides the order of the themes, that is: „coincidental, mechanical, physical, chemical, organic, psychic, ethical, religious, ingenious," and the natural scientist fills this structure with content."[16]

Goethe's Faust and Emanuel Swedenborg

In this regard, it should be noted that, in writing his tragedy, *Faust*, Johann Wolfgang von Goethe is said to have been influenced by the visionary Emanuel Swedenborg, a mystical predecessor of Lorber. To make one

thing clear from the outset, it must be added here that simply the enormous scope of Swedenborg's legacy and Lorber's writings make it nearly
impossible to gain a clear overview that would allow a comparison of the
two. A thorough study of either of these two mystics would take an entire lifetime. However, in Goethe's poetry it is possible to trace detailed
lines of thought that originated with Swedenborg. Gerhard Gollwitzer
(June 7, 1906-March 3, 1973) accomplishes this in his book: *Die Geisterwelt ist nicht verschlossen, Swedenborgs Schau in Goethes Faust* ("The
Spirit World Is Not Closed Off, Swedenborg's Vision in Goethe's Faust").

Gollwitzer was a deeply religious man and Emanuel Swedenborg was
among those who had a great influence on him. He was evidently an ex-
pert authority on Swedenborg's works, which allowed him to detect clear
traces of Swedenborg's messages in Goethe's poetry. In meticulous and
objective juxtaposition, he comments on the sublime poetry of Goethe's
Faust. In the first chapter, Gollwitzer writes:

> Even though the influence of Herder and Lavater on Goethe's development
> has been emphasized, the fact that they themselves were inspired by Sweden-
> borg has generally been overlooked.[17]

According to Gollwitzer, Swedenborg had an influence:

> … on many important people, such as Goethe and the Romanticists, for
> example, Schelling and Jean Paul, on Lavater and Oberlin, and also on Balzac,
> who called him the "Buddha of the North," on Helen Keller – "O light bringer
> to my blindness!" – in Germany's Swabia on Oettinger and Gustav Werner,
> the founder of the Reutlingen Bruderhaus foundation.[18]

Very few Goethe researchers have traced Swedenborg's influence on
Goethe's life and work. This is partly due to the fact that Goethe himself
rarely mentioned Swedenborg by name, even though he remained influenced by Swedenborg's thinking until his death. In his final conversation
with Johann Peter Eckermann, Goethe even quoted Swedenborg literally. Unlike in England and America, where there are large Swedenborg
communities, Swedenborg had remained largely unknown in Germany,
due to his ostracism by Immanuel Kant. This great German philosopher
had reviled and denounced Swedenborg, which may, understandably,
have been the main reason for Goethe's restraint. However, Professor
Gollwitzer was able to prove in his book that Kant in fact revered Swe-

denborg's teachings. Gollwitzer's conclusion as to Kant's inquiries about Swedenborg: "a reasonable, pleasant, and open-hearted man."[19]

Here is a quotation from Goethe that was published in the *Frankfurter Anzeigen*, a literary periodical, at the conclusion of his review of Lavater's *Aussichten in die Ewigkeit* ("Prospects of Eternity"):

> We wish him intimate communion with the worthy seer [Swedenborg] of our times, around whom was the joy of heaven, to whom spirits spoke through all senses and limbs, in whose bosom the angels dwelt ...[20]

Testimonials to Emanuel Swedenborg

It is worth mentioning that Swedenborg's personage and name were known worldwide. The mystic was also admired by many prominent people as a Christian visionary. He was acknowledged as a spiritual scientist of high standing and a thoroughly honest and credible person who was the essential spiritual leader of his time. All this was in keeping with the reputation that preceded this Scandinavian visionary.

Dr. Martin Luther King, Jr.

> "Swedenborg enables us to understand why we were created, why we are alive and what happens to us after our bodies die. Swedenborg enables us to have the best possible understanding of God's message as it exists in those Bible Books which constitute God's Word."[21]

Heinrich Heine

> Swedenborg is a thoroughly honest soul, and his reports about the other world are credible ... This great Scandinavian visionary understood the unity and indivisibility of our existence, just as he correctly recognized and acknowledged the inalienable rights of the individuality of man. Our continuance after death is not some idealized masquerade, in which we put on a new jacket and a new person; both person and costume remain unchanged.

> Heinrich Heine in the epilogue to Romanzero[22]

Carl Gustav Jung

> A visionary of unmatched fruitfulness is Emanuel von Swedenborg (1689–1772), a learned and spiritually elevated man.[23]

Honore de Balzac

> My religion is Swedenborgianism, which, in a Christian sense, is merely a re-
> petition of older ideas. For although religions take on an infinite number of
> forms, neither their meaning nor their metaphysical constructions have ever
> changed. After all, man has always had only one religion. Swedenborg takes
> what Magic, Brahmanism, Buddhism, and Christian mysticism, these four
> great religions, have in common, what is real and divine about them, and, in
> a manner of speaking, provides mathematical justifications for their tea-
> chings.
>
> (Honoré de Balzac in *Louis Lambert*)

Swedenborg can be considered to be the spiritual ancestor of Jakob Lorber.
Lorber was familiar with portions of Swedenborg's writings and there are
many parallels between Lorber's and Swedenborg's writings. In Lorber's
writings, Jesus described Emanuel Swedenborg as wise and his messages as
good and true. Unfortunately, Lorber, Mayerhofer, and, consequently, the
New Revelation have not become as well known as Swedenborg.

Goethe's "Faust"

Johann Peter Eckermann (Sept. 21, 1792–Dec. 3, 1854) was a German
poet, author, and close confidant of Goethe, serving as his secretary. His
transcripts of his conversations with Goethe during the latter years of
Goethe's life brought Eckermann widespread recognition and earned
him great acclaim.

On Monday, June 6, 1831, Goethe showed Eckermann the beginning
portion of the fifth act of Faust, which had at that point not yet been
written. They talked about Faust, whose inherited character trait, dis-
content, has not abated, even in old age.[24]

In Goethe's conception, Faust is intended to be precisely one hundred years old in the fifth act, and he remarked: "I rather think it would
be well expressly to say so in some passege."[25] They then discussed the
conclusion and Goethe drew Eckermann's attention to the passage in
which he had written:

Delivered is the noble spirit
From the control of evil powers;
Who ceaselessly doth strive will merit
That we should save and make him ours:
If Love celestial never cease
To watch him from the upper sphere;
The children of eternal peace
Bear him to cordial welcome there.[26]

"In these lines," said he [Goethe], "is contained the key to Faust's salvation. In Faust himself there is an activity which becomes constantly higher and purer to the end, and from above there is eternal love coming to his aid. This harmonizes perfectly with our religious views, according to which we cannot obtain heavenly bliss through our own strength alone, but with the assistance of divine.

You will confess [so Goethe to Eckermann] that the conclusion, where the redeemed soul is carried up, was very difficult to manage, and that I, in such supersensual matters about which we scarcely have an intimation, might easily have lost myself in the vague, if I had not, by means of sharply-drawn figures, and images from the Christian church, given my poetic design a desirable form and substance."[27]

Gollwitzer explains, as can also be read in the New Revelation, that according to Swedenborg, death is the transition from the bondage of humans to the earthly-physical sphere to the other dimension.

Man does not die, but rather is separated from the physical body [from matter] that had served him well in the world. Man himself lives, for it is not the body that allows him to be man, rather it is the spirit. When he dies, he passes from one world to another.[28]
The external, the body, is designed to be beneficial in the natural world. When a person dies, this is discarded. In contrast, the internal, the spirit, is designed to be beneficial in the spiritual world, and this never dies.[29]

Goethe concludes his *Faust* with Swedenborg's vision:
All of the transient,
Is parable, only:
The insufficient,
Here, grows to reality:
The indescribable,
Here, is done:
Woman, eternal,
Beckons us on.[30]

Artistic Talent and Science

Now, with respect to Goethe, we may justifiably be reminded of Heisenberg, who, since his youth, had always been enamored of Goethe's philosophy of life and his poetry. In particular, he was very familiar with *Faust*, and the story obviously resonated deeply with him. In this regard, we do not need to explicitly point out that Heisenberg's mindset and, evidently, also his religious awareness were influenced by Goethe, which is of course already indirectly conveyed in the introduction to *Reality and Its Order*. It must be remembered that Heisenberg was a superb pianist. In his youth, he was therefore confronted with the difficult decision of whether to study music or physics. This sensitive giftedness he possessed allows us to understand how he was able to interconnect the harmonious tones of Goethe's poetry with his own brilliant philosophy. Heisenberg's unique worldview was, of course, also shaped by his phenomenal scientific insights. The paradigm shift in physics, coupled with his own research and findings from scientific collaboration with contemporary colleagues, molded and renewed not only his own worldview, but also that of many other physicists.

In his book, Heisenberg traverses the various domains of reality, structuring human life from birth to death. He contemplates the fact that reality becomes altered several times in life, beginning in childhood. In this respect, he believes that in our productive years, when, for adults, our world undergoes hardly any change at all, new experiences can still bring about a sudden and uncanny transformation of our reality.

> Where once a meaningful coherence held our life together, there is now a rigid law that decides only according to cause and effect without concern for connections on a higher plane. In earlier times people used to say that God could forsake a human being. But perhaps in our time there are many for whom the world puts on a gray and rigid face.[31]

In the chapter titled "The Creative Forces," he writes about the different layers of reality and the value and meaning of human love. He demonstrates, among other things, his deep understanding of language. At the end of the second part of chapter I, in which he writes about language, he explains:

Every domain of reality can finally be depicted in language. The abyss that separates different domains cannot be bridged by logical reasoning or coherent linear development of language. The ability of human beings to understand is without limit. About the ultimate things we cannot speak.[32]

Through Mayerhofer, Jesus explains:

"Now it so happens that your language, however cultivated and rich in expressions you imagine it to be, so far has no words for many feelings and emotional states which you try to express, as for instance in the most sublime moments of the highest ecstasy of first love, or of farewell or reunion, or even when you want to give verbal expression to harmonic chords and sounds. How much you would then like to express in a word! However, your language has to be satisfied at most with a look full of bliss, a handshake, an embrace. For your words are too poor and unable to express in the least what stands written in flaming letters of spirit in your soul and culminates in the word 'love,' but cannot be described exactly."[33]

"Objective" and "Subjective" – the Parts of a Polarity's Whole

The term "polarity" refers to a philosophical relationship between *two mutually dependent* values. The poles are the two opposite ends of a single object, inseparably bound together *as a single unit* on account of their mutual dependency. "Day" can therefore only be defined in opposition to "night," "hot" only when there is also "cold," "poverty" cannot exist without "wealth," etc.

At the end of Chapter I, 3, Heisenberg discusses the terms "objective" and "subjective." From his philosophical perspective, he defines and classifies them as the two sides of a single object: "from which an order of reality can take its beginning."[34] I believe that here, Heisenberg is deliberately avoiding reference to a philosophical relationship such as would be understood in dualism, in which everything breaks down into *two mutually exclusive properties* (to the point of incompatibility). Heisenberg writes:

They also describe two sides of reality itself. Still, it would be a crude oversimplification to divide the world in an objective and a subjective reality. This merely black and white representation created much inflexibility [concepts] in philosophy of the last few centuries [e.g. in dualism, for instance, in the example of "good" and "evil"].[35]

Emotion and Reason

I find it a very subtle task to assign the conceptual properties of "subjective" and "objective" to a generic term at the scientific level as well. Heisenberg does indeed demonstrate that "polarity" explains oppositions between different characteristics, but also that the properties of the poles do, in fact, belong to a single reality. As is easily seen, Heisenberg assigns "subjective" to emotion and "objective" to reason; in his view, these poles are always mutually dependent.

Because Lorber sometimes received his revelations about nature as allegories and analogies, some scientists are unable accept them unless they can tap into their heart's innermost feelings.

> Jesus saith: "1. Behold, small is the heart of man, but the greater the horizon of his feelings, such a one is in the power of faith out of pure love for Me. I tell you, there is no thing so hidden that it does not wish to be reached by the rays of pure emotion; and when the pure rays of emotion have then grasped something, ask yourselves whether it would still be possible to grasp the thing differently from what it really is and exists in itself. 2. Quite different, of course, is the case with men of understanding. They scrabble with this short hand [of understanding] after all things, just as young children scrabble after the moon and other very distant objects. These people then draw their emotions into their narrow minds and let them grope about in these haughty ones, like a blind man who has sat down on a block of stone carved over with hieroglyphics and grabs around on it, without even a slight suspicion attempting to whisper to him that these are actually hieroglyphics, and, even less, that this writing is a mysterious language corresponding to the bright rays of pure emotion. 3. Behold, so it is also with these, My communications and revelations of My grace given to you. If you will examine and illuminate them with the rays of your emotions, their truth will immediately become clear to you, and you will find yourselves suddenly feeling as if the matter had been known to you for the longest time. But if you look at them with your intellect, they will begin to seem more and more foreign to you; for, as I have said, the intellect has only very short arms, which are also very weak, and therefore it is not able to reach great things, even if they were to be very close to it, and even less to reach distant things, and then to draw them to itself – and then even, to pull suns into its narrow snail-shell for the blind touching of its chastened emotion. 4. Behold, that is not at all possible. And since the mind must become aware that such things are impossible, it becomes angry, leaves everything behind, removes all unnecessary objects from its snail-shell and is satisfied with its own abstractions, finally even bidding farewell to the chastened

emotion, becoming colder than the North Pole itself, and beginning, in its supreme stupidity, to marvel at itself as a god, where it does not even worship itself, since it has at last come so far that it begins to realize that it knows nothing, and yet, in this not-knowing, imagines itself to know everything. That is then finally the greatest triumph, yea, a triumph, for which the most innocent child would not give a penny – and of which every angel, no matter how humble, is repulsed. 5. Therefore, you, too, are to completely imprison your intellect in obeisance to pure emotion within a living faith borne out of love for Me [thus, do not subordinate your intellect to obedience to blind faith, for this would mean the death of the intellect], then you will see all things as they are; and only then will you begin to see clearly and distinctly where the eternal sun of truth and reality shines. 6. This little is told you so that you may know in the future by what measure My revelations are to be judged. Amen."[36]

Determinacy and Coincidence – versus – Human Free Will

Heisenberg shows that an individual process cannot be called a perception unless there is a fixed chain of cause and effect between people. For the process that takes place during the course of interpersonal communications, for example, this basis does not exist. In his discussion on coincidence, Heisenberg shows that, in contrast to the ideal state defined by classical physics, in which what happens in space and time during natural processes is completely fixed (determinacy[37]), quantum theory introduces an entirely new situation.

> In place of the closed system as something that happens in space and time, there is the totality of possible space-time processes that takes place when a system is under observation, that is to say, when it is in connection with the external world.[38]

In experimental findings in quantum mechanics, Heisenberg excludes an *observable*, effective law of nature. Within these experiments, the results are left to chance by the interrelationships of fixed frequencies [probability].

> Rather, what takes place is left to the play of chance (within the range of frequency determined by those connections). In this domain, chance may initially be understood as "purposeless;" that is how Goethe too perceived the word chance in the section of his Theory of Color referred to. After all, the

word "purpose" envisages a direct relation to us as thinking and suffering beings about whom we cannot yet speak here, where we are occupied with laws of nature.[39]

He therefore considers that the events, which here seemingly take place by chance, might be determined by different and overriding laws of nature. Because the laws of quantum theory have been confirmed many times, this would be unlikely. However, the situation would be quite different if we had knowledge of systems in which the conceptual conditions of quantum theory cannot be applied. The probability statements would no longer be fixed and could therefore be subordinated to interrelationships of a completely different kind.

> In this sense, and in this sense only, one may say that today physics leaves open the possibility that certain processes that appear to follow the play of chance in light of nature's laws known to us, are perhaps determined by connections of a higher order.[40]

What Heisenberg means by this, is that the determination of this question must be left to experience in each individual case. As a comparison, he points to the randomness found in the formation of crystals, when drops of water solidify in the cold air to form snow crystals.

In Heisenberg's opinion, since experience has not provided us any evidence that the formation of snow crystals, in our example, is bound to any specific shape by higher-level interrelationships, we are permitted to believe in the game of chance. He simultaneously clarifies that there is no obligation to come to this conclusion, since we do not really have any knowledge of the quantum-theoretical state of the water drop before or during crystal formation. Heisenberg ponders:

> Even if we believe that the growth of an individual crystal was not predetermined, so that another, somewhat different one could have developed just as easily, nothing has been decided about whether the coincidence to which the crystal owes its form was "purposeless." For a crystal's formation is an irreversible historical act which as such can also play an important role in the context of our lives or that of the world, even if it was not predetermined. Contexts of a kind that justify us to use the word "purpose" can also be connected to events which could just as well have transpired differently without any reason whatsoever. [41]

Einstein's dogma, that "the Old One does not play dice" has therefore not been refuted. Indeed, it was shown that the Creator's plans are not carried out on the basis of pure chance, but that by incorporating certain freedoms, God has executed His plan for pure happiness. The discussion in this chapter, in particular, proves that Heisenberg was able to show that, in the cosmic order, coincidences certainly do intervene in events. In doing so, he made it clear that this can also occur without the external influence of observable laws of nature. Heisenberg illustrates this with the creation of atoms, in which many perfect physical states materialize as matter. Their always precise structure can be observed in the many millions of divine masterpieces in nature. It is interesting to note that he wrote elsewhere that throughout the universe as well as here on earth, chaotic states independently orient themselves toward the central order.[42]

In my opinion, this inimitable perfection of the world as a whole is proof as to why God has no need to intervene in (determine) earthly events. At the same time, it also makes clear that all organic elements of the earth are able to evolve freely. Just as Heisenberg correctly recognized that, in the cosmic order, coincidences are not only permissible but also effective, so it is also understandable that in our case, human free will is firmly anchored in the divine order of things. If we consider this a bit more precisely, we quickly come to the conclusion that without this rule of the divine order, neither the previous nor any future evolution of humanity would make any sense.

From Mayerhofer's *The Lord's Sermons*:

As the seed of a tree carries within it all the nuclei for its future destination, thus My Word, which as a product of My Spirit keeps producing something new incessantly, never passes but continues forever. Therefore, John said: "In the beginning was the Word ... and the Word was God!" I, too, am the seed out of which continuously and everlastingly only the divine can go forth. Wherever this Word falls as a seed, it stimulates the ground to activity – often permanently, often only temporarily.

However, since I am also the sower who sows the seed all over the entire creation, it naturally also happens that – as in the parable – not all the seed develops equally. One brings more fruit, the other less and the third none at all. Firstly, because even the worlds of My creation, together with their dwellers, are not all on the same level and, secondly, because everywhere men have their free will to act in whatever way they see fit. Hence the different spiritual results in all the worlds and with all human beings and the different lengths of road all created beings have to travel to reach their destination of the spiritualization of their souls.[43]

Organic Life

In the section of the book in which Heisenberg discusses "the structure of the biological domain," he is critical of the theory of evolution and its explanation regarding the origins of life. In particular, he sees the term "law" as problematic in a discussion of biological processes:

> [...] since a natural law is by its very nature a statement about processes that can be repeated as often as one wishes. [...]In any case, biology for now refers to organic life on our earth. Laws can therefore be spoken about in as many places as there are repeatable biological experiments. But these experiments always presuppose the existence of life as it has developed. The origin of living organisms from inorganic matter remains a unique historical process.[44]

In another passage, he writes:

> [...] that the laws we are looking for and their action cannot be limited to the living substance but that they must be about quite general connections that touch all that happens and – as follows from the concept of law – are generally binding.[45]

Mayerhofer was permitted to reveal this:

> "Yes, My children! There is a higher life, a life that reaches far beyond all that is transient and even in the rock is infinite. For also the rock changes only its form and chemical structure, but it too does not become nothing, and whatsoever is infinite in the rock, owing to its origin from Me, which in the plant and animal kingdom and in the human race is even more distinctly expressed, this imperishable something is the bond uniting the material with the spiritual world, and both with Me!"[46]

Access to Creative Forces

In the chapter in which Heisenberg describes the special position held by human beings, he reflects on a further, higher stage in human evolution.

Before discussing the concept of consciousness, he contemplates the unimaginable periods of time during which human evolution will take place. Taking the human embryo as an example, he concludes that although during the first few weeks it externally displays only the features of this early stage of development, it is already unconsciously participating in the higher-level interrelationships that are embodied only in humans. Heisenberg wrote that the potential for human development expresses itself in the embryonic stages, but it is in the nature of things that we do not have language that would allow us to speak about this evolution.

> After all, a language can only be formed for that part of reality where our life takes place. What is at issue here may be summed up in the following somewhat unclear statement: In contrast to all other living beings on our earth, the human being is the only one possessing access to the creative forces.[47]

In keeping with the second of Heisenberg's thoughts, Mayerhofer, in his *Secrets of Life*, some seventy years before Heisenberg, was allowed to proclaim:

> However, since I am infinite and, as Creator, must be thus, it is natural that nothing that was created could ever be faulty or have shortcomings, for the fault would be just as infinite as the principle according to which it was created. Thus, no object created by Me allows for an actual improvement or ennoblement, but certainly for a perfecting process gradually leading to ever higher levels of development, which process has already been predestined and well-planned in the first embryo.[48]

Consciousness

I may be mistaken, but in my view, now, at the very latest, it becomes clear that Heisenberg's remarks were actually not exclusively about mathematical probabilities, i.e. coincidences in quantum theory or the inadequacies of everyday language. It would appear that he wanted to emphasize that the higher domains of reality are objectively too sharply delineated, so that therefore, presumably no one has yet dared to define the boundaries of these domains and their mutual relationship to one another. The reason for this, as he states, is because all previous studies have nearly always had to limit themselves to describing and classifying only events that can be experienced. According to Heisenberg, determining how higher domains of reality are related to lower domains, seeing them against this backdrop, would require overcoming an almost impenetrable darkness. Because the next higher level of reality in organic life is the existence of consciousness, a conscious life.

> Given that the connections between an individual's life and her or his consciousness are so close, one has to ask whether one may meaningfully separate consciousness and life into two domains at all. On the contrary, there are many indications that these are effects of the same kind which relate the parts of an organism to a common, integrated whole and which may manifest themselves in consciousness as wishes of feelings, impressions or acts of the will.[49]

After providing us with easily understood explanations on his thoughts about the relationship between consciousness and unconscious processes in the human brain and how these thoughts ultimately led him from these electrochemical functions to the comparison with quantum theory, Heisenberg explains:

> Now, even though it appears certain that we are able to describe a constant flow from the fully conscious processes of the mind to the wholly unconscious action of the organic creative forces, it leaves wide open the question as to whether the actual cognitive situation of observing consciousness is not fundamentally different from that of observing life.[50]

Heisenberg repeatedly notes that our ability to adapt is greatest during childhood. However, only as our growth process approaches its end do we become mature enough to allow certain focused, vibrant connections to develop. Only then can we integrate ourselves into our surroundings or form a connection with another person.

> [...] the emergence of such a living connection is so sudden, so much something that happens to us without notice and as if by a higher power, that it can fill us with something like a deep and holy terror. It is as if the divine itself had come down to earth and were speaking to us through just that human being or landscape. What takes place here in detail is something that only the poet can describe in parables, for no one who has encountered God at this place would dare talk in ordinary language about that event. But what is certain is that behind the reality of such a living relationship the entire rest of the world taken in by the senses loses its force for a long time, either by receding into the shadows or by being enfolded into and taking part in the radiance that now floods all of consciousness.[51]

Symbols and Shapes

In a previous chapter, there was a discussion of how, in personal prayer or meditation involving an image of the resurrected Lord's shroud, individual symbols or emblems can become visible on the Shroud. From the author's point of view, some symbols can help people transcend the limits of what can be perceived by our human senses. She herself has discerned symbols on the Shroud of Christ as emblems and believes these to be messages from God.

Heisenberg writes:

> At the gate that leads from the domain of simple consciousness to the field of the mind and everything connected to it stands the "symbol." However little we know for now about this array of connections, it may even be justified to gather up in this word symbol the entire domain of reality which is to be depicted as a cohesive configuration above and beyond simple consciousness. For everything of the mind, whether in language, science or art, rests on the use of symbols and their power. Matters of the mind are not tied to bodies but are transmitted through symbols.[52]

In defining humankind, Heisenberg drew on the creation of symbolic forms, because in his opinion, all subsequent evolution can only begin from the layer of reality in which there are symbols.

> For life in itself is dim and **only the power to create symbols and to understand them turns us from living beings into human beings.**[53]

He also shows that by using symbols in a specialized way, their meaning and intellectual content can be communicated. The way in which symbols in the arts and sciences are organized makes their meaning comprehensible. We see examples of this in the arts in the form of musical notation and in science with mathematical symbols.

In the process, he explains that mathematics and the humanities share a common fundamental property in that their content is entirely within the domain of reality, but this reality has only been created through the existence of symbols.

The Symbols of the Human Communities

This chapter contains an explanation (which I have greatly condensed) from Heisenberg that the merging of large communities always takes place under certain symbols. He names, among other things, the cross, which, since the end of antiquity, has held together the cultural sphere of the Western world.

The Creative Forces

> Having said all this, now we must finally turn to the highest layer of reality where those parts of the world come into view of which one can only speak in parables. We could begin by telling a parable and talk about the layer of reality which connects us to eternity.[54]

But because parables would not yet make sense here, Heisenberg wants to once again look back and refer to the stepladder that connects the domains of reality and that ends at the uppermost layer of reality. He repeats that the order or map of the domains was meant to replace the rough division of the world into an objective and a subjective reality between two poles.

Because his wording might be misunderstood, Heisenberg seeks to explain the relationship between facts and knowledge referred to here in terms of the domains of reality that have already been presented.

> We know that among human beings love exists; one can also often speak of it as of any objective state of affairs. But we have also experienced that the relationship to another human being can be a very tender creation which can be altered be being affected by any word or even any idea.[55]

The remaining pages of this chapter reveal the distinctive mindset of a great scientist. What is particularly impressive is Heisenberg's responsible approach. He explains that the color and brightness of the objects around us, as can be detected with optical devices, is not dependent upon us. However, whether we see the world in bright colors or whether it appears to be gray-on-gray to us is determined by our attitude toward others and by our state of consciousness. This means, as he says, that this aspect of reality often carries far more weight for the entirety of human destiny than does any objective aspect.

> Happiness and unhappiness are only slight dependent upon objective, external events. Our happiness requires certain preconditions in our soul and not merely favorable external circumstances. Love makes the soul grow wings, writes Plato in Phaedrus.[56]

According to his insights, this internal attitude toward the world determines our thinking and actions and thus indirectly extends into the objective realm. However, this attitude, in turn, depends decisively on the processes of cognition, the manner in which this perception enters our consciousness. Attitudes are so different from person to person that this aspect can no longer be objectified. As one possible example of this, he uses the case of a situation in which we find ourselves in a state where we feel as though we are separated from the world by a veil of mist, and how then even just a sympathetic question from a friend, asking if we are alright, transforms this state into another state. Heisenberg describes the two following facts as being initial characteristic features of the reality layer:

> First, reality is dependent to a significant extent on the condition of our soul, that therefore we are ourselves able to transform the world. Second: the effect of this ability to change, nonetheless partially diminishes objectification because, for one, human beings happen to be different and relate differently to the world and, for another, this creative condition of the soul is part of the sea of unconscious soul-processes and cannot be raised up to the surface of consciousness without being altered.[57]

In the second point, he sees another dependency, because if we maintain that we can transform the world through the powers of the soul, then we must also maintain that we cannot transform the world according to our will. Even through the most acute exertion of our forces of will, none of us can succeed in creating a relationship with another person that we would refer to as love. Quite the contrary, our instinct would tell us that the will is a totally unsuitable vehicle for dealing with that part of our soul in which the decisive changes in reality occur.

> However, the human ability to understand is unlimited; therefore, there are also ways for consciousness to exert influence on the soul's creative powers. Religious teachings, for example, at the heart of which is contemplation, contain explicit direction on how people are to comport themselves in order to preserve and strengthen the soul's powers. Probably part of every ethic is basically also a collection of such instruction designed to keep the soul healthy.

Only the superficial observer thinks of moral law as an impediment to the individual's life in favor of the community, as a restriction of freedom. For the thoughtful person, it is the collection of ancient insights into how we ought to conduct ourselves in order – as the ancients use to say – "to be happy" or, in Christian terminology: "to find mercy in the eyes of God" or, in terms of what we are addressing here: "to safeguard the soul's creative powers." It will be conceded that these three formulations basically mean the same.[58]

In the following three sub-sections I will let the quotations speak for themselves. Heisenberg's self-explanatory thoughts essentially fulfill in many ways the revealed wishes of God that Mayerhofer was allowed to record in the sermon on the greatest commandment. As mentioned previously, we were particularly impressed by the high sense of responsibility reflected in what Heisenberg, as a scientist, left to his fellow human beings as reading material, and not only in his essay. Up to a ripe old age, he continued to give many public readings and interviews in which he presented his principles of reality to interested lay audiences.[59]

Religion

All religion begins with the religious experience.[60]

We might say, for example, that we suddenly became aware of the connection to another, higher world, in a way that committed us for the rest of our life, or that in a certain situation, God met and spoke to us directly. (I myself would think here first of all of that summer-night in 1920 on the balcony of the Pappenheim Ruin.) We could also put it like this: The meaning of life suddenly became clear to us and now we know how to distinguish with certainty between what is of value and what is not. "Whoever once circled the flame always shall follow the flame,"[61] –becoming aware of the other, higher world is something that happens to us quite unexpectedly, from the outside, as it were, so that we can have no doubt whatever that all of a sudden another world stands there before us and claims us.[62]

While the real religions again and again direct attention inward and strive to keep the creative domain of the soul as free of injury as possible in spite of all the misfortune in the world, the world-view devoted to the objective leaves the soul defenseless before every monstrosity. The damage done in this process may be even greater because it normally does not enter people's consciousness. That is why it is improbable that this world-view will be able to prevail in the long run, in case the words of Christianity eventually become incomprehensible altogether. Instead, another language will have come into being in which the forces will again be named explicitly that transform the world through our souls.[63]

Spiritual Enlightenment

It is not by our will that love and "the other world" come to us. We can perhaps make ourselves receptive to their coming, we can wish that they would come, or have given up every hope for their appearance. Be that as it may, wherever they touch our lives we must simply accept them as a gift, without asking whence they came, as the grace of a higher power that determines our fate and to which we may gratefully submit.[64]

This reminds us finally that the creative powers manifest themselves in yet another form. It happens explicitly in this ultimate, most decisive place and only to the one graced human being, namely where we speak of spiritual illumination or of the inspiration of the genius. In all ages, people have seen it this way whether one speaks like Plato of divine madness, or human beings were taken to be the tool or envoy of God, or whether the ingenious man or woman was revered as a special kind of human being, as was the case in the nineteenth century. It was always acknowledged that without willing it, power flowed into rare individuals to capture in symbols what is intransient, to make God's action known in their time and in so doing, to intervene for centuries in humankind's fate, fortune, or misfortune.[65]

Also, the task is always openly acknowledged with the maturing of consciousness and made into the plumb-line of life regardless of the sacrifices required. Those with whom this happens are, after all, no longer merely human beings; rather, they are workshops in which the creative powers are visibly at work, creating testimonies that point beyond everything belonging to the human sphere. What takes shape in this highest layer of reality is at one and the same time the most objective and the most subjective: the most objective because the persons in question are aware at every moment of creativity that they are acting at the call of another world that is creating through them, and the most subjective because in each instance, what has been brought into being could be said, written or thought in this particular way only by this one human being.[66]

The Great Parable

Everything that has been said here can also be framed as a discussion of the perennial question about the existence of God. As it has sought to answer that question, human thought has taken many steps, each of which is essential in order to reach the next.[67]

One can speak about the ultimate ground of reality only in terms of parable and when people say parabolically "I believe in God, the Father," then this god really directs the destinies of human beings like a father through their faith. This faith is no self-deception but simply the conscious acceptance of the ever irresolvable tension in reality which surely is "objective" and runs its course independently of us humans. And yet again, it is also only the content of our soul, and it is transformed from within our soul.[68]

The question of the existence of God has long ceased to be a scientific question; it is a question of what we are to do. But that is always very simple even as times change. We are to be active members of human society, helping others and being diligent about it. Thus, in the symbols of the community the foundation of the world remains alive and fruitful to which we feel we belong as harmonious members. And this blossoming in the world, which is at the same time "God's world," finally also remains the greatest happiness the world is able to offer: namely the consciousness of home.[69]

Today, I realize that it is necessary to have absorbed a few chapters of the fascinating Goethe-Heisenberg texts to be able to understand that Heisenberg's writings were about far more than what the average interested layperson would suspect. No further commentary is needed on Heisenberg's intellectual work. The number of topics in his writings that I have yet to read gives me the sense that I am not yet finished with the unique worldview of this great scientist and his religion and philosophy. This brilliant scientist presented his orderly view of the world and reality in such a way (if I, as a philosophical layperson, can judge this at all) that it is equal parts the language of an objective scientist and that of a man of deep integrity.

With his profound explanations of his views and his superb choice of words, Heisenberg demonstrates to us his great sense of responsibility as a scientist. Nevertheless, we would like to mention something that we find somewhat sad: namely, that even in his later years, Heisenberg himself never published this essay. However, if we consider the social consequences of such a decision for renowned scientists, it becomes evident why almost every brilliant researcher, at least during their professionally active period, keeps private any emotional insights that point to God. They otherwise run the risk that a considerable portion of their life's work would then be judged to be ambiguous, even in retrospect.

As a whole, some aspects of our personal reality are therefore better left unspoken. In my opinion, Heisenberg's lectures and writings clearly show that he wanted to preserve his status as a physicist for the sake of posterity. From my point of view, he succeeded masterfully and with bravura. His final, brief Chapter III, which he left untitled, is, in a way, a declaration of his personal convictions.

You can clearly sense in his words the terrible effect that Heisenberg's experiences in the Second World War had on him. Twenty-five years earlier, as a youth, he had been forced to experience wartime. From his point of view, it was impossible in the political sphere to avoid the struggle between one set of spurious ideals pitted against another set of spurious ideals. When it came to shaping the future of the world, Heisenberg believed that science would play an increasingly important role, because it is the point where people are confronted with the truth.

> Most important are therefore particularly those areas of pure science in which practical application is irrelevant but rather where pure thought is searching out the hidden harmonies of the world. That innermost realm, where science and art are almost indistinguishable, is perhaps the only place where humankind today meets truth, totally pure and no longer veiled by human ideology and desire. True, the great masses of people nowadays have just as little access to this realm as people in earlier times had to the inner sanctum of the temple. But the masses are quite content to know that some people are entering that realm and that there deception is not possible because **there the Good Lord decides.**[70]

He thought that the verses of Stephen George's poem were applicable to humanity as a whole, quoting only the beginning line: "Whoever once circled the flame ..."[71] explaining that, in a certain sense, what used to take place among primitive tribes is now largely being repeated.

Although against his own will, the scientist has become the people's magician to whom the forces of nature are obedient. But his power can turn to good only when he is at the same time a priest and acting merely as mandated by the deity or by fate.[72]

---

1   https://youtu.be/d5eMSvMQ020 (accessed 26 October 2020)
2   Duerr, Hans Peter, *Physik und Transzendenz*, p. 18. Translation by C. Dyre.
3   Barnett, Lincoln: *The Universe and Dr. Einstein*, https://archive.org/stream/TheUni-

verseAndDrEinstein/Barnett-TheUniverseAndDrEinstein_djvu.txtt, p. 95. (accessed Oct. 26, 2020)

4 Ibid.

5 Ibid.

6 Einstein, Albert, *The World As I See It.* General Press, New Delhi, 2018, p. 45.

7 Ibid., p. 148

8 Ibid.

9 Einstein, Albert, *"Science, Philosophy, and Religion, A Symposium,"* published by the Conference on Science, Philosophy and Religion in Their Relation to the Democratic Way of Life, Inc., New York, 1941, https://www.sfheart.com/einstein. html (accessed Oct. 26, 2020)

10 Heisenberg, Werner, *Der Teil und das Ganze – Gespräche im Umkreis der Atomphysik* (Physics and Beyond: Encounters and Conversations), pp. 120-121. Translation by C. Dyre.

11 Ibid., p.250

12 Mayerhofer, Gottfried, *The Lord's Sermons.* Translation by the author.

13 Heisenberg, Werner, *Der Teil und das Ganze*, p. 250. Tautology refers to a statement that is always true, independent of the truth value of the underlying components. Translation by C. Dyre.

14 Ibid., pp. 252, 253.

15 Heisenberg, Werner, *Reality and Its Order*, Konrad Kleinknecht (Ed.), M.B., Rumscheidt, N. Lukens, I. Heisenberg (Transl.) Springer Nature Switzerland AG, 2019, p. 13.

16 Ibid.

17 Gollwitzer, Gerhard: *Die Geisterwelt ist nicht verschlossen, Swedenborgs Schau in Goethes Faust*, p. 7. Translation by C. Dyre.

18 Ibid.

19 Ibid., p. 8, as well as in Gollwitzer's remarks 1–3 on p. 63.

20 http://www.swedenborg.finden-und-kennenlernen.de/swb 10000.htm (German - language only).

21 M.L. King Jr. Library: https://coolwisdombooks.com/incredible-cures-ignored-by-science-royal-rife-and-others/

22 Translation by C. Dyre.

23 In: *Die neue Kirche: Monatsblätter für fortschrittliches religiöses Denken und Leben*, September 1947, p. 86. Translation by C. Dyre.

24 Eckermann, Johann Peter, *Conversations of Goethe with Eckermann and Soret*, Band 225 von Johann Wolfgang von Goethe, p. 399. https://books.google.de/books?id= ZuAIAAAAQAAJ&printsec=frontcover&redir_esc=y#v=onepage&q&f=false (accessed Nov. 4, 2020)

25 Ibid.

26 Ibid., p. 400

27 Ibid.

28 Gollwitzer, Gerhard: *Die Geisterwelt ist nicht verschlossen, Swedenborgs Schau in Goethes Faust*, p. 445. Translation by C. Dyre.

29   Ibid., p. 224

30   https://www.poetryintranslation.com/PITBR/German/FaustIIActV.php#Act
     _V_Scene_I (accessed Oct. 28, 2020)

31   Heisenberg, Werner, *Reality and Its Order*, p. 21.

32   Ibid., p. 29

33   Mayerhofer, Gottfried, *Secrets of Life*, p. 492.

34   Heisenberg, Werner, *Reality and Its Order*, p. 34.

35   Ibid.

36   Lorber, Jakob, *Himmelsgaben,* Vol. 3, Ein kurzes Beiwort zur Darstellung des Sudpols.
     Die Größe des Menschenherzens, Gefühl und Verstand. October 16, 1840, pp. 65,
     1–66, 6. Translation by C. Dyre. Please also refer to p. 108 in the chapter "Connections
     Between the Shroud, the New Revelation and the Gospels."

37   Determinacy: A complete ascertainment of what is happening in space and time; this
     would exclude randomness. In philosophy, it is the determination or dependence of
     the (non-free) will.

38   Heisenberg, Werner, *Reality and Its Order*, p. 63.

39   Ibid., pp. 63-64

40   Ibid., p. 64

41   Ibid., p. 65

42   Heisenberg, Werner, *Der Teil und das Ganze*, p. 252. For Pauli, Heisenberg's concept of
     truth and his mental model of the central order is understandable, but he asks: „But
     what do you mean by that [...] what do you mean by enforcing? Heisenberg answers:
     "I mean something quite banal, for instance, the fact that after every winter, flowers
     bloom once again in the meadows and that after every war, cities are rebuilt, that
     chaos always transforms into order." [Ibid.]

43   Mayerhofer, Gottfried, *The Lord's Sermons.*

44   Heisenberg, Werner, *Reality and Its Order,* pp. 74-75.

45   Ibid., pp. 76-77

46   Gottfried Mayerhofer, *Secrets of Life*, p. 331, iBook.

47   Heisenberg, Werner, *Reality and Its Order,* pp. 82-83.

48   Mayerhofer, Gottfried, *Secrets of Life,* p. 285, iBook.

49   Heisenberg, Werner, *Reality and Its Order*, p. 83.

50   Ibid., p. 84

51   Ibid., p. 87

52   Ibid., p.89

53   Ibid., p.92

54   Ibid., p.107

55   Ibid., p. 108

56   Ibid.

57   Ibid., p.109

58   Ibid.

59   An internet search for "Werner Heisenberg" yields numerous publications.

60   Heisenberg, Werner, *Reality and Its Order*, p. 110.

61 George, Stefan: "The Star of the Covenant" in *Poems – Rendered into English; Pantheon Books, Inc. 1943, p. 210*, quoted by Heisenberg in *Reality and Its Order*, p.110.

62 Heisenberg, Werner, *Reality and Its Order*, p. 110.

63 Ibid., p. 113

64 Ibid.

65 Ibid., p. 114

66 Ibid., p. 115

67 Ibid., p. 116

68 Ibid., pp. 116–117

69 Ibid., p. 118

70 Ibid., pp. 120–121

71 see Endnote 61

72 Heisenberg, Werner, *Reality and Its Order*, p. 121.

Reflections of the Co-Author

Tangible, Because It Is Illuminating

As is well known, the writings of prominent scientists often contain noteworthy information about their phenomenal insights. The more extraordinary the mysteries of nature, the more extraordinary the personal worldviews of their discoverers. The same type of information is often also contained in biographies of researchers that include personal information about them. In any case, when reading such texts, I was often left with the same impression. As soon as the limits of genius have been reached or even exceeded, researchers turn to God's Creation. Not often, but occasionally, God is openly and truthfully named as the Originator. It is interesting to note that it is these researchers in particular who have made significant progress in their field.

In my search for such finds, my initial intention was therefore only to learn more about the knowledge these genius researchers had acquired. I was no longer interested in scientific justifications based on objective evaluations, nor in extraordinary insights or laws of nature constructed on the basis of these insights. For one thing, these matters can only be understood within the limits of our own personal experience. Second, it was never our intention to present a treatise on innumerable scientific laws of nature. On the contrary, from the time I first became acquainted with the Shroud messages, I, as co-author, already had a feeling of certainty, and this feeling became more intense and persistent through my work with the Shroud images.

The easily comprehensible explanations in the New Revelation were equally effective in generating my awareness. Up to now, the well-balanced and consistently objective language of those texts of the New Revelation that I have been able to delve into generate a sense of peace within me. Even after only a few pages, these texts reveal the sustaining forces underpinning the stable foundation of God's all-embracing Creation. The most essential underlying element in the Creation of the earth and the universe, and the basis for every living being that exists, is understood to be the ever-perceptible love of God.

Ideally, our love of others should be guided by the way we love ourselves or want to be loved. The commandment to love our neighbor is that by which God measures our love for Him. Compassion, sympathy, empathy, and kind, caring generosity all embody that which human dignity itself comprises. This element, which is actually not difficult to comprehend, reveals the magnificence of the Divine order. Divine Love is the epitome of Creation. Acknowledgment of this and the observation of this great God-given commandment encompass all the principles of Christian virtues. Without this love of neighbor, it would be inconceivable for humanity to successfully co-exist.

An additional crucial fundamental element is the free will that God has entrusted to us humans. He gives us this freedom so that our souls may achieve perfection. This allows us to accept all of God's commandments without fear. As is also explained in the New Revelation, our Creator does not, of course, want us to become automatons, because this would negate the purpose and future of His creation. Jesus repeats to Lorber, in abridged form:

> This is a matter of the greatest necessity on that globe on which men are destined to become true children of God by their own effort! If I in the least limited man`s freest will, this would totally ruin My purpose! (GGJ 3, 177, 1–10)

With love and understanding we thus voluntarily move toward God. "Toward God" was also Max Planck's guiding watchword in his never faltering, ceaseless battle against skepticism and dogmatism, against unbelief and superstition, a battle that Religion and Science are waging together, now and throughout future ages.[1]

We would be very pleased, dear readers, if our book has allowed you to recognize the connection between the messages of the New Revelation and those of the Shroud. Because this strong connection between the Christian messages can also be linked to the respected views of distinguished scientists, this bond represents a unique unanimity.

This balanced interaction can enable the development of a mature belief system. For scientists who see themselves as responsible for the human community, this connection can also generate a sense of peace. If the central convictions and thought processes are linked together, scientific insights into the cosmic order will complement each other and expand far beyond our ability to experience the laws of nature. These interconnections within reality also strengthen our sense of neighborly love and, thus, our steadfast faith in God.

As you may have noticed as you read this book, the selected quotations from the scientists were primarily on an emotional level. The proportion of scientific, technical, and theoretical information was kept to an absolute minimum. The intellectual portion that dealt with the theoretical knowledge of the natural sciences as a whole was, on the whole, presented in a condensed and broadly comprehensible form. Even if the concept of dematerialization through the dissolution of Jesus' body after his death or the enigmatic nature of His shroud brought some quantum-theoretical phenomena to mind, any attempt to resolve these enigmas would have defeated our original goal. That is why our Shroud messages, as is actually recommended in the New Revelation, are based on the feelings that we perceive as reality.

Dear reader, I hope that some of the messages in this book have been helpful in answering some of the important questions you have in your own life. It would be wonderful if, as I myself was able to feel while writing this book, you, too, were able to experience a comforting and reassuring certainty. I wish you all the best always!

Warmly,

Peter Kutzki

---

1   Duerr, *Physik und Transzendenz*, p. 39.

Epilogue by the Author

Dear Readers,

Often, we take note of many of the things that we perceive in everyday life without evaluating or critiquing them. For me, reading, in the figurative sense of our human perception, means making an unerring selection, taking in the indisputable parts of the thoughts expressed in order to draw the most accurate conclusions possible. With symbols, we are dealing with a different situation as regards our potentialities. Symbols are a short-cut means of communicating complex information. They help people transcend their own individual views, i.e. to go beyond the limits of what is perceptible to the senses. For me, the most important signal in Jesus' Shroud messages is the "3" in the three furrows of his forehead, which I have hopefully adequately and comprehensibly discussed in the third chapter. And so, with divine help, every individual has the ability form their own opinion, understand these matters, and expand the knowledge they themselves need.

The artistic depiction of the Transfiguration of Christ in St. Apollinare in Classe is unique and a work of absolute genius. "Evil" and human cruelty have no place in the mosaics of Ravenna and, in contrast to God, are given no opportunity to unfold. This mosaic art conveyed to me an authentic picture of Christianity as taught by Jesus himself in the New Revelation. The early Christian world of images reflects the stories of Jesus' life, prophetically laid down in idyllic, paradisiacal and superlative fashion. In the overall composition of the "Transfiguration of Christ on Mt. Tabor" in St. Apollinare, the most important figures in the history of Salvation are depicted. With Jesus, Michael, Gabriel, Elijah, Moses, and the four evangelists, "Heaven," i.e. the spiritual world, descends gently, golden and full of love, upon the earth. The face of Christ on the cross, positioned at the center of the circle of stars, is a heavenly representation of the divinity of Jesus. Just gazing at this generates a feeling of being ceremoniously and lovingly welcomed into this heavenly community.

A very different feeling arises when learning of the clear-cut insights and courageously expressed worldviews of renowned scientists. In particular, the scientists referred to in this book are the ones who have attributed the laws of nature on earth and in the universe as well as the cosmic order to the Creator. Together with the Shroud messages and the New Revelation, this creates a vast spiritual space in which I can, even for eternity, feel at home and secure.

In this book, it was therefore my desire to encourage you, dear reader, to re-examine some of the information you may have encountered or read in your own search for God. Our book is meant to be a useful and helpful source of inspiration in your search for God. And so, for this reason, I do not want to forego the opportunity to describe, in my closing chapter, what it was that so deeply moved me personally years ago and that helped me most in my own search for God. I am always happy to retell the story of this personal experience and to recommend it, because it opens the door to wonderous and beautiful experiences for everyone.

If you, too, have felt an inner desire, then try to establish a personal connection to Jesus Christ by way of His image. What I suggest you do to establish direct contact with our heavenly Father is to enter into contemplative devotion, using the Shroud image in all of its original and variously handed-down forms. As I have shown, we human beings need this trusting and intimate connection with the Spirit of Christ to be a nurturing companion throughout our life's journey. Because God helps us when we ask Him, prayer is a particularly worthwhile activity for us children of God.

After all, prayers are also meant to allow us to relieve some of the pressure we feel on our souls. The fact that God meets us with His generous love provides us with a unique opportunity. As for me, I believe that He knows how we are doing and what our worries and concerns are. Despite our weaknesses, He stays by our side and protects our lives, our thoughts, and our prayers.

God truly is good to us and taking the time to speak to Him inwardly leads to the joyful experiences with which God wants to bless us. I don't think it matters whether you focus on the Shroud of Christ or simply close your eyes and thank God. Often, it is the silent and reverent loving prayers that are the best suited for seeking divine guidance. I wish you wondrous success on your search and many moments of happiness!

Yours in Christ,   *Gisela Elisabeth Heinz*

Closing Thoughts – In Goethe's Words

To conclude, we would like to leave you with a passage from Eckermann's book, recounting one of his conversations with Goethe concerning true religion. In his journal entry from Sunday, March 11, 1832, Eckermann wrote quite impressively and enlighteningly about Goethe's character and special worldview:[1]

> This evening for an hour with Goethe, talking of various interesting subjects. I had bought an English Bible, in which I found, to my great regret, that the apocryphal books were not contained. They had been rejected, because they were not considered genuine and of divine origin. I greatly missed the noble Tobias, that model of a pious life, the Wisdom of Solomon, and Jesus Sirach,– all writings of such high mental and moral elevation, that few others equal them. I spoke to Goethe of my regret at the very narrow view by which some of the writings of the Old Testament are looked upon as immediately proceeding from God; while others, equally excellent, are not so. As if there could be anything noble and great which did not proceed from God, and which was not a fruit of his influence.
>
> "I am thoroughly of your opinion," returned Goethe. "Still, there are two points of view from which biblical subjects may be contemplated. There is the point of view of a sort of primitive religion, of pure nature and reason, which is of divine origin. This will always be the same, and will last and prevail as long as divinely endowed beings exist. It is, however, only for the elect, and it is far too high and noble to become universal. Then there is the point of view of the Church, which is of a more human nature. This is defective and subject to change; but it will last, in a state of perpetual change, as long as there are weak human beings. The light of unclouded divine revelation is far too pure and brilliant to be suitable and supportable to poor weak man. But the Church steps in as useful mediator, to soften and to moderate, by which all are helped, and many are benefited. Through the belief that the Christian Church, as the successor of Christ, can remove the burden of human sin, it is a very great power. To maintain themselves in this power and in this importance, and thus to secure the ecclesiastical edifice, is the chief aim of the Christian priesthood.
>
> "This priesthood, therefore, does not so much ask whether this or that book in the Bible greatly enlightens the mind, and contains doctrines of high morality and noble human nature. It rather looks upon the books of Moses, with reference to the fall of man and the origin of a necessity of a Redeemer; it searches the prophets for repeated allusions to Him, the Expected One, and re-

gards, in the Gospels, His actual earthly appearance, and His death upon the cross, as the atonement for our human sins. You see, therefore, that for such purposes, and weighed in such a balance, neither the noble Tobias, nor the Wisdom of Solomon, nor the sayings of Sirach, can have much weight. Still, with reference to things in the Bible, the question whether they are genuine or spurious is odd enough. What is genuine but that which is truly excellent, which stands, which stands in harmony with the purest nature and reason, and which even now ministers to our highest development! What is spurious but the absurd and the hollow, which brings no fruit – at least, no good fruit! If the authenticity of a biblical book is to be decided by the question, – whether something true throughout has been handed down to us, we might on some points doubt the authenticity of the Gospels, since those of Mark and Luke were not written from immediate presence and experience, but, according to oral tradition, long afterwards; and the last, by the disciple John, was not written till he was of a very advanced age. Nevertheless, I look upon all the four Gospels as thoroughly genuine; for there is in them the reflection of a greatness which emanated from the person of Jesus, and which was of as divine a kind as ever seen upon earth. If I am asked whether it is in my nature to pay Him devout reverence, I say – certainly! I bow before Him as the divine manifestation of the highest principle of morality. If I am asked whether it is in my nature to revere the Sun, I again say – certainly! For he is likewise a manifestation of the highest Being, and indeed the most powerful which we children of earth are allowed to behold. I adore in him the light and the productive power of God; by which we all live, move, and have our being – we, and all the plants and animals with us. But if I am asked – whether I am inclined to bow before a thumb-bone of the apostle Peter or Paul, I say – "Spare me, and stand off with your absurdities!"

"'Quench not the spirit,' says the Apostle. There are many absurdities in the propositions of the Church; nevertheless, rule it will, and so it must have a narrow-minded multitude, which bows its head and likes to be ruled. The high and richly-endowed clergy dread nothing more than the enlightenment of the lower orders. They withheld the Bible from them as long as it was possible. Besides, what can a poor member of the Christian Church think of the princely magnificence of a richly-endowed bishop, when he sees in the Gospels the poverty and indigence of Christ, who, with his disciples, travelled humbly on foot, whilst the princely bishop rattles along in his carriage drawn by six horses!"

"We scarcely know," continued Goethe, "what we owe to Luther, and the Reformation in general. We are freed from the fetters of spiritual narrow-mindedness; we have, in consequence of our increasing culture, become capable of turning back to the fountain head, and of comprehending Christianity in its purity. We have, again, the courage to stand with firm feet upon God's earth, and to feel ourselves in our divinely-endowed human nature. Let mental culture go on advancing, let the natural sciences go on gaining in depth and breadth, and the human mind expand as it may, it will never go beyond the elevation and moral culture of Christianity as it glistens and shines forth in the Gospel!

But the better we Protestants advance our noble development, so much the more rapidly will the Catholics follow us. As soon as they feel themselves caught up by the ever-extending enlightenment of the time, they must go on, do what they will, till at last the point is reached where all is but one.

The mischievous sectarianism of the Protestants will also cease, and with it the hatred and hostile feeling between father and son, sister and brother; for as soon as the pure doctrine and love of Christ are comprehended in their true nature, and have become a vital principle, we shall feel ourselves as human beings, great and free, and not attach especial importance to a degree more or less in the outward forms of religion. Besides, we shall all gradually advance from a Christianity of words and faith, to a Christianity of feeling and action."

The conversation turned upon the great men who had lived before Christ, among the Chinese, the Indians, the Persians, and the Greeks; and it was remarked, that the divine power had been as operative in them as in some of the great Jews of the Old Testament. We then came to the question how far God influenced the great natures of the present world in which we live?

"To hear people speak," said Goethe, "one would almost believe that they were of opinion that God had withdrawn into silence since those old times, and that man was now placed quite upon his own feet, and had to see how he could get on without God, and his daily invisible breath. In religious and moral matters, a divine influence is indeed still allowed, but in matters of science and art it is believed that they are merely earthy, and nothing but the product of human powers.

Let any one only try, with human will and human power, to produce something which may be compared with the creations that bear the name of Mozart, Raphael, or Shakespeare. I know very well that these three noble beings are not the only ones, and that in every province of art innumerable excellent geniuses have operated, who have produced things as perfectly good as those just mentioned. But if they were as great as those, they rose above ordinary human nature, and in the same proportion were as divinely endowed as they. And after all what does it all come to?

God did not retire to rest after the well-known six days of creation, but on the contrary, is constantly active as on the first. It would have been for Him a poor occupation to compose this heavy world out of simple elements, and to keep it rolling in the sunbeams from year to year, if he had not had the plan of founding a nursery for a world of spirits upon this material basis. So he is

now constantly active in higher natures to attract the lower ones."
Goethe was silent. But I cherished his great and good words in my heart.

---

1   *Conversations with Goethe with Eckerman and Soret*, Vol. 2, John Oxford. Smith (Transl.), Elder & Co, London. 1850, pp. 421–426. https://books.google.de/books?id =ZuAIAAAAQAAJ&hl=de&pg=PA426#v=onepage&q&f=false (accessed Nov. 10, 2020)

"Corona," another word for "Crown"

Christ's Crown of Thorns – a Symbolic Message?

Jesus says:
The evolution of Christianity will be an allegory of my life.

Wearing a crown of thorns, Christ died on the cross from asphyxiation and a ruptured heart.

Those infected by the corona virus can die painfully from lung and heart failure.

[13]If I shut up heaven that there be no rain, or if I command the locusts to devour the land, or if I send pestilence among my people; [14]If my people, which are called by my name, shall humble themselves, and pray, and **seek my face**, and turn from their wicked ways; then will I hear from heaven, and will forgive their sin, and will heal their land.[1]

---

1   Chronicles: 7:13–14

Bibliography

On the internet, you will find almost all relevant studies on the Shroud under www.shroud. com. "The Shroud of Turin Website" is maintained by STERA, the "Shroud of Turin Education and Research Association." In several languages, the publications and events on the Shroud are constantly updated and kept up to date.

Many videos on the subject, including popular science videos, can be found on YouTube in various languages. The work of Petrus Soons, who created a 3D model of the Crucified, is very moving.

Barnett, Lincoln: *Einstein und das Universum.* With a forward by Albert Einstein. Frankfurt am Main: Fischer, 1956.

Barrow, J. D., Tipler, F. J.: *The Anthropic Cosmological Principle.* Oxford: Clarendon Press, 1987.

Brown, Simon: *The Shroud of Turin Speaks for Itself* 1st Edition, 2013 www.theupperroomfellowship.org/shroud-turin-speaks/

Bulst, Werner: *Das Grabtuch von Turin: Zugang zum historischen Jesus? Der neue Stand der Forschung.* Karlsruhe: Badenia Verlag, 1978.

Bulst, Werner, Pfeiffer, Heinrich: *Das Turiner Grabtuch und das Christusbild. Band 1: Das Grabtuch: Forschungsberichte und Untersuchungen.* Frankfurt am Main: Verlag Josef Knecht, 1987.

Bulst, Werner: *Betrug am Turiner Grabtuch. Der manipulierte Carbontest.* Frankfurt am Main: Verlag Josef Knecht, 1990.

Bulst, Werner, Pfeiffer, Heinrich: *Das Turiner Grabtuch und das Christusbild. Band 2: Das echte Christusbild: Das Grabtuch, der Schleier von Manoppello und ihre Wirkungsgeschichte in der Kunst.* Frankfurt am Main: Verlag Josef Knecht, 1991.

Bustachini, Gianfranco: *Ravenna, Die Mosaikhauptstadt.* Ravenna: Verlag Salbaroli, undated.

Calaprice, Alice (Ed.): *Einstein sagt – Zitate, Einfaelle, Gedanken.* Munchen: Piper, 2001.

Die neue Kirche: Monatsblaetter fur fortschrittliches religioeses Denken und Leben

Duerr, Hans-Peter (Ed.): *Physik und Transzendenz. Die grossen Physiker unseres Jahrhunderts ueber ihre Begegnung mit dem Wunderbaren.* Bern: Scherz Verlag, 1986.

Duerr, Hans-Peter: *Gott, der Mensch und die Wissenschaft.* Augsburg: Pattloch, 1997.

Duerr, Hans-Peter, YouTube video: Wir erleben mehr als wir begreifen [2018].

Eckermann, Johann Peter: *Gespraeche mit Goethe,* Dr. Erich Regen (Ed.). Berlin: Verlag A. Weichert, 1913.

Eckermann, Johann Peter: *Conversations with Goethe,* John Oxford. Smith (Transl.). London: Elder & Co, 1850.

Eggenstein, Kurt: *The Unknown Prophet Jakob Lorber,* Violet Ozols (Transl.). Salt Lake City: Merkur Publishing Inc., 1979.

Eggenstein, Kurt: *Der unbekannte Prophet Jakob Lorber. Eine Prophezeiung und Mahnung fuer die naechste Zukunft.* Bietigheim: Lorber Verlag, 5. Auflage 2005.

Engel, Leopold: *Johannes – das grosse Evangelium. Empfangen vom Herrn durch Jakob Lorber.* Band 11. Bietigheim: Lorber Verlag, 1987.

Einstein, Albert: *Aus meinen spaeten Jahren.* Stuttgart: Deutsche Verlagsanstalt, 1979.

Einstein, Albert: *The Human Side. New Glimpses from his Archives*, Helen Dukas and Banesh Hoffmann (Eds.) Princeton: Princeton University Press, 1979.

Einstein, Albert, Infeld, Leopold: *Die Evolution der Physik.* Reinbek bei Hamburg: Rowohlt, 1987.

Einstein, Albert, *The World as I See It* (Transl. Alan Harris), https://play.google.com/store/books/details?id=Y_9kDwAAQBAJ&rdid=book-Y_9kDwAAQBAJ&rdot=1&source=gbs_vpt_read&pcampaignid=books_booksearch_viewport (accessed November 12, 2020).

Einstein, Albert, in the "Pfarrnachrichten der katholischen Probstei Werl" from January 1, 2015.

Fanti, Giulio: *La Sindone una sfida alla scienza moderna.* Rome: Aracne editrice, 2008.

Fanti, Giulio: "Beschaedigungsfreie Datierung von antiken Leinengeweben mittels vibratorialer Spektroskopy." In *Vibration Spectroskopy,* Vol. 67, July 2014, pp. 61–70.

Fanti, Giulio: "Interview." In *Vatican Insider*, February 25, 2014.

Frossard, Andre: *Il vangelo secondo Ravenna.* Torino: Societa Editrice Internationale, 1995.

George, Stefan: *Werke.* Vol. I: *Der Stern des Bundes.* Stuttgart: Klett-Cotta, 1984.

Gollwitzer, Gerhard: *Die durchsichtige Welt. Ein Swedenborg- Brevier.* Zuurich: Swedenborg Verlag, 1975.

Gollwitzer, Gerhard: *Die Geisterwelt ist nicht verschlossen. Swedenborgs Schau in Goethes Faust.* Zuurich: Swedenborg Verlag, 2nd edition, 1998.

Grossheim, Antonie: *Die sieben Worte Jesu Christi am Kreuz. Als inneres Wort empfangen.* Bietigheim: Lorber Verlag, 8th edition, 1960.

Heisenberg, Werner: *Schritte uber Grenzen, Gesammelte Reden und Aufsaetze.* Munich: Piper, 1984

Heisenberg, Werner: *Physik und Erkenntnis 1927–1955. Ordnung der Wirklichkeit, Interpretation der Quantenmechanik, Atomphysik, Kausalitaet, Unbestimmtheits-Relationen und mehr.* Collected Works, Vol. 1. Munich: Piper, 1984

Heisenberg, Werner: *Ordnung der Wirklichkeit,* Munich: Piper, 1989.

Heisenberg, Werner: *Der Teil und das Ganze. Gespraeche im Umkreis der Atomphysik.* Munich-Berlin: Piper, 13th edition, 2017.

Heisenberg, Werner: *Quantentheorie und Philosophie, Vorlesungen und Aufsaetze,* Jurgen Busche (Ed.). Stuttgart: Reclam, 2018.

Herrmann, Joachim: *Astronomie die uns angeht,* Ruediger Proske (Ed.). Guetersloh: Bertelsmann, undated.

Kowalska, Maria Faustyna: *Tagebuch der Schwester Maria Faustyna Kowalska aus der Kongregation der Muttergottes der Barmherzigkeit.* Hauteville: Parvis-Verlag, 1993.

Kupsch, F. R.: *Lehrbuch und Atlas Der Anatomie. Nervensysteme – Sinnesorgane.* Vol. III. Leipzig: Georg Thieme, 1943.

Lebensgarten, Reichstes Betrachtungs-Buch, zusammengestellt aus neuen Eroeffnungen des Herrn.
Part B (3 Parts.). Reprint of the 1899 edition. Bietigheim: Lorber-Verlag, 1991

Lindner, Eberhard: *Das Grabtuch Jesu, Zeuge der Auferstehung. Das entschluesselte Geheimnis von weltgeschichtlicher Bedeutung.* Karlsruhe: Martha Lindner Verlag, 2009.

Lorber, Jakob, Mayerhofer, Gottfried: *Lebensgarten Ein Betractungsbuch in drei Teilen.* Bietigheim, Lorber Verlag: undated.

Lorber, Jakob: *Von der Hoelle bis zum Himmel. Die jenseitige Fuehrung des Robert Blum.* Bietigheim: Lorber Verlag, 3rd edition, 1963.

Lorber, Jakob: *Johannes das grosse Evangelium.* Vols. 1–10. Bietigheim: Lorber Verlag, 8th edition, 1986.

Lorber, Jakob: *Die Wiederkunft Christi. Ein Entwicklungsbild der Menschheit.* Bietigheim: Lorber Verlag, 4th edition, 1989.

Lorber, Jakob: *Himmelsgaben.* Nachdruck der Auflage von 1935, Bietigheim: Lorber-Verlag, 3rd edition, 1990.

Lorber, Jakob: *Briefwechsel zwischen Abgarus Ukkama, Furst von Edessa, und Jesus von Nazareth.* Bietigheim: Lorber Verlag, 10th edition, 1994.

Lorber, Jakob: *Die drei Tage im Tempel. Gespraeche des zwoelfjahrigen Jesus.* Bietigheim: Lorber Verlag, 10th edition, 1995.

Lorber, Jakob: *Die geistige Sonne. Mitteilungen uber die geistigen Lebensverhaeltnisse des Jenseits.* Bietigheim: Lorber Verlag, 7th edition, undated.

Lorber, Jakob: *Die Jugend Jesu. Das Jakobus-Evangelium.* Bietigheim: Lorber Verlag, 11th edition, 1996.

Lorber, Jakob: *Schrifttexterklaerungen: Bibeltexte und ihr geheimer Sinn.* Bietigheim: Lorber Verlag. 6th edition, 2000.

Malfi, Pierandrea: *La Sindone: primo secolo dopo Cristo!* Edizioni Segno. (English: *The Shroud of Turin: First Century after Christ!* Hoboken: Pan Standford, 2015)

Mayerhofer, Gottfried: *Lebensgeheimnisse, Eroeffnungen ueber wichtige Lebensfragen. durch das Innere Wort empfangen von Gottfried Mayerhofer.* Bietigheim: Lorber Verlag, 1981.

Mayerhofer, Gottfried: *Schoepfungsgeheimnisse. Kundgaben ueber Dinge der Natur. Durch die innere Stimme des Geistes empfangen von Gottfried Mayerhofer.* Bietigheim: Lorber Verlag, 1989.

Mayerhofer, Gottfried: *Secrets of Life,* Translator unknown. EPUB book, downloaded from https://archive.org/details/6.ebooksecretsoflife (accessed November 12, 2020).

Mayerhofer, Gottfried: *Predigten des Herrn. Durch das innere Wort erhalten und niedergeschrieben.* Bietigheim: Lorber Verlag, 2003.

Moretto, Gino: *Das Grabtuch, Anleitung.* Editrice Elledici, Turin 2000

Pfaffenzeller, Wilhelm: *Die Irrtuemer der Religionen und Wissenschaften fuehren zur Selbstvernichtung der Menschheit.* Bietigheim: Turm Verlag, 1976.

Planck, Max: *Physikalische Rundblicke. Gesammelte Reden und Aufsaetze.* Hirzel, Leipzig, 1922.

Planck, Max: *Sinn und Grenzen der exakten Wissenschaft.* Lecture held in Nov. 1941. Leipzig: J. Barth Verlag, 1965

Planck, Max: *Vortraege und Erinnerungen.* Darmstadt: Wissenschaftliche Buchgesellschaft, 1970.

Planck, Max: *Vortraege, Reden und Erinnerungen*, Armin Hermann and Hans Ross (Eds.). Berlin: Springer, 2001

Kopsch, Fr., Rauber, August: *Lehrbuch und Atlas der Anatomie des Menschen*, Vol. III *Nervensystem – Sinnesorgane*, 16th edition, Leipzig: Georg Thieme Verlag, 1943.

Resch, Andreas: *Das Schweißtuch von Oviedo*. www.imagomundi.biz/resch/andreas-resch-das-schweißtuch-von-oviedo [Accessed on November 13, 2019]

Scheuermann, Oswald: *Das Tuch. Neuste Forschungsergebnisse zum Turiner Grabtuch*. Regensburg: Pustet Verlag, 3rd edition, 1987.

Scheuermann, Oswald: *Turiner Tuchbild aufgestrahlt? Nachweisversuch*. Saarbruecken: Verlag Dr. Muller, 2nd edition, 2007.

Siliato, Maria Grazia: *Und das Grabtuch ist doch echt. Die neuen Beweise*. Augsburg: Pattloch Verlag, 1998.

Stuehlmeyer, Barbara, Karl Braun: *Das Turiner Grabtuch. Faszination und Fakten*. Kevelaer, Butzon und Bercker Verlag, 2018

Swedenborg, Emanuel: *Wahre christliche Religion. Enthaltend die ganze Theologie der Neuen Kirche*. Zurich: Swedenborg Verlag, undated.

Swedenborg, Emanuel: *Kurze Darstellung der Lehre der Neuen Kirche*. Zurich: Swedenborg Verlag, 2nd edition, undated.

EMANUEL SWEDENBORG und seine geistige Ausstrahlung, Lebenslauf. Broschuere Selbstverlag Woldemar Kiefer, Zurich: Hausdruckerei Swedenborg Verlag, 1974.

Tipler, F. J.: *The Physics of Christianity*. New York, London ...: Doubleday, 2007.

Waldstein, Wolfgang: *Neueste Erkenntnisse ueber das Turiner Grabtuch. Auch Atomforschung erweist Echtheit. Farbreportage uber die Turiner Brandkatastrophe*. Stein am Rhein: Christiana Verlag, 1997.

Wesselow, Thomas de: *Das Turiner Grabtuch und das Geheimnis der Auferstehung*. Munich: C. Bertelsmann Verlag, 2013.

Wilson, Ian: *Das Turiner Grabtuch. Die Wahrheit*. Munich: Goldmann Verlag, 1999.

Zehetbauer, Markus: *Jesus? Die Ergebnisse der Grabtuchforschung*. Planegg: Promultis Verlagsbuchhandlung, 1988.

List of Illustrations

About the Authors

Gisela-Elisabeth Heinz, born in 1952, grew up in Hamburg, Germany. After completing her training as a dental technician, she studied Dentistry. In her own dental practice, she also worked as a naturopath. After her marriage to her late husband, she continued her practice in Upper Bavaria until 2018. Her interests include people, religions, and health, especially when approached from a spiritual point of view. She is a member of the Catholic Women's Association. She particularly enjoys reading a wide range of non-fiction books, outdoor sports, painting icons, gardening, and spending time in nature.

Co-author Peter Kutzki was born in 1950 in Starnberg am See, Bavaria, Germany, where he grew up, taking an early interest in science and philosophy. He completed training as a building services technician before marrying his wife Susanne in 1972 and welcoming his son Sven in 1973. In 1977, he launched his own business as a master craftsman. He enjoys drawing and reading philosophical writings, particularly those of  Arthur Schopenhauer and Dr. Gustav Grossmann. In 1990, he made a career move to the industrial sector as a consultant for burner and heating technology. Following the death of his late wife, he began working on the manuscripts for this book.